THE BEAULIEU RIVER GOES TO WAR
1939 - 45

BY
CYRIL CUNNINGHAM

Montagu Ventures Limited
John Montagu Building
Beaulieu
Brockenhurst Hampshire SO42 7ZN

First published by Montagu Ventures Limited 1994

ISBN 0 9523386 0 2

© Cyril Cunningham 1994

The right of Cyril Cunningham to be identified as the author of this work has been asserted by him in accordance with the Copyright, Design and Patents Act 1988

All rights reserved. No paragraph of this publication may be reproduced, copied or transmitted save with written permission or in accordance with the provisions of the Copyright, Design and Patents Act 1988, or under the terms of any licence permitting limited copying issued by the Copyright Licensing Agency 90 Tottenham Court Road, London W1P 9HE

Any person who does any unauthorised act in relation to this publication may be liable to criminal prosecution and civil claims for damages

Printed in the United Kingdom

Acknowledgements
The author and publishers are grateful to the following for permission to reproduce photographs (listed alphabetically by source and numerically by figure number):

K. Adams from the RB Adams Collection: 2
Mr. Owen Aisher: 49
Associated Press Photos: 51
Myles Cooper: 11
Hugh Cowin/TRH Pictures: 42
Crown Copyright Office: 15
Miss Joan Firth: 55, 56
Mrs. S. Graham: 3, 34, 57
C.D. Mitchell: 20, 22, 23
Mudge (Fawley Historians): 30
National Motor Museum: 8, 9, 19, 43.
Ocean Images (UK) Ltd. 60.
Royal Marines Museum: 50
Southampton City Museum
/Hallett-Jerrard Collection : 44, 46.
Mrs. Stobart: 24
Weidenfeld & Nicolson: 28

The following photographs are Crown Copyright, The Imperial War Museum, London (listed numerically by figure numbers followed by their negative numbers):
10 (HV1337), 12 (A24495), 13 (H20214)
14 (A12357), 16 (A23759), 17 (HU 1905)
18 (A24493), 26 (A27944), 27 (A23440), 31 (A23673)
32 (A24017), 33 (H32052), 35 (HU1916), 36, (A24092),
37 (Neg. No. not known), 38 (A23754), 39 (A23606),
40 (A23591), 41 (A23276), 45 (A23725)
47 (A28017), 48 (A23749), 53 (A23685).

The following photographs were taken by Mary Cunningham or by the author or were taken from the author's collection: 1, 4, 5, 6, 7, 21, 25, 29, 54, 58, 59.

Every effort has been made to contact holders of copyright material. However, if any have been inadvertently overlooked the publishers will be pleased to make the necessary arrangements at the first opportunity.

ii

ACKNOWLEDGEMENTS

My heartfelt thanks and lasting gratitude are due to Lord Montagu for rescuing and publishing this book after it had been turned down by twenty seven publishers on the grounds that it was of 'too local' interest to justify publication.

I also have to thank several members of the staff of Montagu Ventures Ltd. for their support and practical assistance, specifically Graham Carter for managing the project, Sue Tompkins for her initial gift of general information about Beaulieu during the war and Judy Davies for very practical help in chasing pictures and copyright holders and for bringing the script and pictures together and seeing them through to print. I also wish to thank Simon Clay for taking additional photographs and for his technical advice, Simon Warne for the cover design and Tim Griffiths for inside design.

My thanks are due to Mr. Edmund and Mr. Lionel de Rothschild for allowing me to read and copy many of the letters of former members of HMS Mastodon who were applying for tickets for the 50th anniversary reunion. Also to Charles Orr-Ewing and Mrs Sheila Piggott of the Exbury Estate Office. It was the information in these letters that inspired me to carry out research into the history of HMS Mastodon.

No history can be written without the help of numerous people. I wish to thank Steven Brooks, Keeper of Military History at the D-Day Museum at Southsea for his unstinting help on a number of occasions over a period of two years and for allowing me to spend many hours in his office reading the Operation Orders for Operation Neptune. Also for allowing us to photograph the Neptune Operation Orders. My thanks are also due to Matthew Little, Librarian of the Royal Marines Museum at Eastney for allowing me access to official documents.

My thanks are due also to Ron Hansford, the librarian of Hythe Public Library for his generous help in tracking down essential books and references and for his encouragement. He also gave me some valuable information about the Free French Forces at Inchmery House.

I would like to thank Air Commodore H Probert for obtaining for me from the Air Historical Branch the official details of the Junkers 188 bomber that crashed on the Exbury estate in April 1944.

I also wish to thank Mr. Owen Aisher, the present owner of Clobb Copse, not only for allowing me into his garden to look at and photograph the oyster beds and the basin where the floating dock was constructed but also for putting me in touch with several very distinguished former members of Coastal Forces.

I also offer my gratitude to my brother in law, John Gulliver, MBE, who spent much of the war in the assault ship HMS Invicta, and with whom I spent many enjoyable hours yarning about his experiences. He was an invaluable source of information about the history of Combined Operations and its activities in the Solent area and he also provided me with eyewitness accounts of several assault landings, including Dieppe and D-Day.

Among the former members of the staff of HMS Mastodon who provided me with information there was one in particular who gave me much help, former Supply Wren Joan Firth, who deserves my special thanks for putting up with my barrage of questioning letters. I have to thank her also for permitting me to use the SSEF signal made after the assault on Walcheren Island. Thanks also to her former colleagues Mr. L.G.Riall BEM and Mr. S.Mead who also helped. Other former Mastodons who provided information were Mrs.P.Egerton, Mrs.M.Mead,

Mrs.E.Smith and Ms.B.Spreadbury; also many thanks to Mrs S.Graham for allowing me visit her home to inspect her very interesting scrapbook and for providing some photographs.

Former Naval officers and ratings whom I wish to thank for providing useful information are Sir Alan Dalton, CBE.,DL., Mr.N.Kitchen and Mr. M.Webb, and Mr. A.J.Billing and Mr.S.Young. Also, my thanks to three former Royal Marines for providing me with valuable information; Mr. S.Taylor for information about Gun craft and Mr.R.Windross about the Ferry Units. Also Mr.J.Jones who was once the Royal Marine bodyguard to Admiral Ramsey.

Finally, I have to thank my wife, Mary, for her encouragement and months of patience with me during the gestation and research period of this book and for her impelling sense of humour through the period of the writing. I also thank her for her sound advice and suggestions about the sequencing and structuring of certain passages and for proof reading several versions of the manuscript.

FOREWORD
by LORD MONTAGU OF BEAULIEU

I well remember my Easter holidays of 1944 when at seventeen years old I was in my last year at Eton. The Beaulieu area and its New Forest surroundings were suddenly designated an area of special security so I was somewhat surprised yet intrigued to be told that I had to have a special permit to come home. In due course a little pink piece of paper was issued which I retain to this day, and I had to produce it at check points when going in and out of the area. Upon returning home I found the Estate literally bristling with troops, who were stationed in the woods and fields, and there was much activity on the River and foreshore, where at Park Farm a temporary airfield had been constructed. I was solemnly warned not to stray down to Buckler's Hard or into the woods, although I did sneak down once or twice where I was faced with the amazing sight of a river full of landing craft and other Royal Naval vessels. There was also enormous activity at Buckler's Hard, where sections of the Mulberry Harbour were being built and Canadian MINCA barges were being assembled, having come over in sections by rail to Beaulieu Road Station. At the end of April I went back to Eton, reluctantly leaving this hive of activity, but because I was at school during May and on D-Day itself, missed the last hectic weeks.

However, I often wondered about the ships on the River and what happened to them and also about the secret weapons designed by Neville Shute which I saw being tested at the mouth of the River. I was therefore delighted to be approached by Cyril Cunningham with a magnificently researched manuscript describing in great detail the history of every vessel that was on the River and the part they played in Operation Overlord and other wartime engagements.

It therefore seemed right that, as a major contribution to the fiftieth anniversary of D-Day, I should take on the responsibility for publishing this book, which clearly shows what an important part the Beaulieu Estate and River, Buckler's Hard and HMS Mastodon at Exbury contributed to the successful landings in Normandy.

Nine houses at Beaulieu were also requisitioned for the training of SOE personnel, some of whom arrived from Occupied Europe and returned there in MTBs stationed in the River and who were to play a vital part behind the lines.

Today, where landing craft nestled in 1944, there are splendid yachts enjoying a peacetime and peaceful river. It should however be remembered that in the 18th century and especially during the Napoleonic wars, the wooden ships built for the Royal Navy at Buckler's Hard played their part in defeating Napoleon, in particular such famous ships as HMS Agamemnon, Nelson's first flagship before he assumed command of HMS Victory. Significantly, in the Second World War Buckler's Hard, the Beaulieu River and Exbury were once again able to play an important part in defeating Hitler. My congratulations to Cyril Cunningham for describing how "The Beaulieu River Goes to War" in such a comprehensive manner and making such an important contribution to the history of World War Two in Hampshire.

Montagu of Beaulieu

CONTENTS

Chapter 1	The Ghosts on the Beaulieu River	1
Chapter 2	Twilight War	6
Chapter 3	Innovation and Experimentation	17
Chapter 4	The Reformation of HMS Mastodon	27
Chapter 5	Nevil Shute and the Mystery Bomber	40
Chapter 6	Neptune's Trident	47
Chapter 7	Westkapelle: The Jaws of Death	56
Chapter 8	Fortunes of War	64
	Bibliography	75
	List of Major Landing Craft using the Beaulieu river 1939 - 45	76
	Index	78

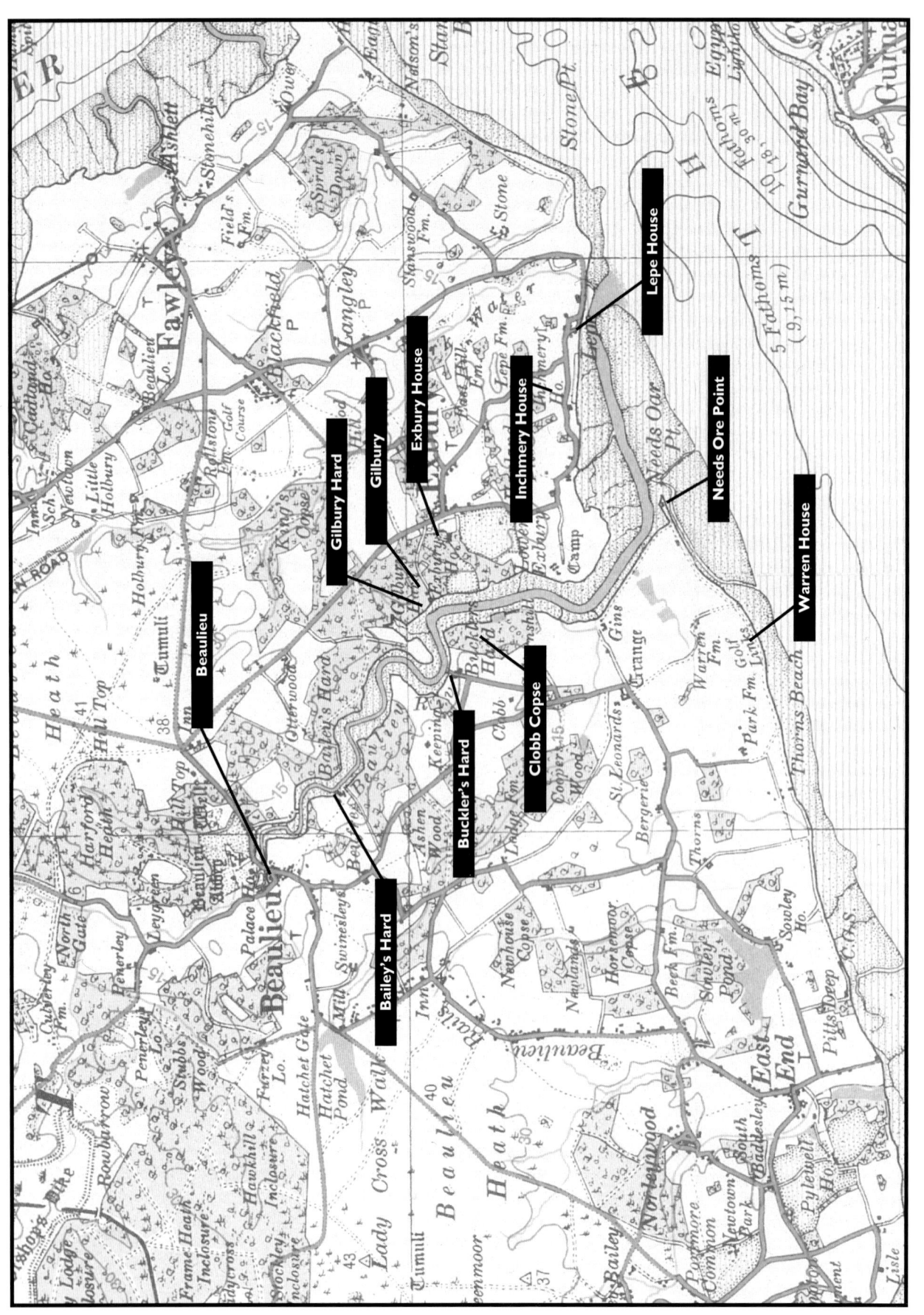

Reproduced from a map of the area printed in Germany in 1938 onto which the key place names referred to in this book have been superimposed

CHAPTER I
THE GHOSTS ON THE BEAULIEU RIVER

In the Spring of 1961, soon after I moved from Berkshire to the Waterside area of the New Forest, near Southampton, I took my family to the nearby Exbury Gardens. We drove past the Lodge and through the main gates of the estate, past a small brick building on the left of the drive, once the guardhouse. There was no sailor standing there now, with a rifle over his shoulder, muffled in his heavy greatcoat, blowing into his mittened hands and stamping his feet to keep warm.

I parked the car on the lawn in front of Exbury House and while my wife attended to the unloading of our two children I rushed across to the House, forlorn and empty now, and stood before it reverently gazing at its desolation. I had last stood here in the winter of 1944 when I had been nineteen years old and a Midshipman, the First Lieutenant of a tank landing craft lying in the Beaulieu river.

My mind became crowded with echoes of the past; the constant traffic of Naval officers and ratings and pretty young ladies of the Women's Royal Naval Service, the Wrens, in the days when it was a stone frigate called HMS Mastodon, immortalised in Nevil Shute's novel "Requiem for a Wren". I wondered how Nevil Shute had come to know so much about Mastodon. Perhaps he had served here. It took me a long time to discover that he had and still longer to find out what he had been doing.

I trailed after my family as they relished the beauty of the gardens on a glorious spring day and suddenly realised that I was registering very little of it because I was preoccupied with my ghosts, the ghosts of a store party of grumbling sailors, dressed in tatty, faded boiler suits, caps awry, struggling under the weight of sacks of potatoes and tinned food and bread, cursing all the way

1. Exbury House (HMS Mastodon)

from the victualling huts at the back of the House and down the long path to Gilbury pier to the trot boat.

My wife could not understand my impatience to go down to the Beaulieu river. When, during our walk down to the water, my eight year old son, hopping and skipping along beside me asked, "What were you doing here in olden days, daddy?" it made me realise that my experiences here, during the second world war, were as remote and alien to his generation as Nelson's days were to mine. They were part of history. The large Gun craft, the Flak craft and especially the Rocket craft, whose terrifying fire power sent 17 tons of explosives flying through the air in a matter of seconds, were gone for ever, long since superceded by modern helicopter gun ships and troop carriers.

But the tank landing craft, once so numerous that they choked the lower reaches of the Beaulieu river, were one of the few enduring legacies of the war. They were the forerunners of today's roll on - roll off ferries. Indeed, a converted Mark 4 LCT plied between Southampton and Cowes long after the war, carrying thousands of holidaymakers, cars and lorries to the Isle of Wight. They called it the Norris Castle, formerly LCT 828, and it was owned by the Red Funnel Steamers.

When we reached Gilbury pier, I looked up and down the river staring in wonderment, stunned by the silence and the tranquility. The yachts and boats worrying their

3. LCVP on the Beaulieu River with Wren crew

moorings in the slight breeze seemed tiny compared with the 500 ton monsters I had known.

Gone were the chapped-faced Wren trot boat crews huddling round a brazier in the mouth of a small brick shed at the start of the pier. Gone were their open 36 ft LCVPs which used to tear up and down the river carrying us and our supplies out to the trots of major landing craft further downstream. Instead there was now a pervading silence where once there had been the incessant whine of generators and the interjecting growls of powerful diesel and petrol engines. Gone, too, was the urgency, the barking of orders, the smell of oil and engine fumes. Gone were the noisy, boisterous sailors, perpetually starved of female company, hurling coarse remarks at the Wren Petty Officer trot boat cox'n, a girl in her early twenties, who ignored the lewd innuendo and studiously avoided showing any preference for young RNVR

2. M.V. "Norris Castle"

officers, to forestall any loud accusatory mutterings of "Officers' mess!"

It took me years to lay my ghosts to rest. Some of them refused to go away because of their exploits. Who, now, would remember the commanders and the heroes of

4. The author as a Midshipman, RNVR

those years; Captain (later Commodore) 'Jock' Hughes-Hallett RN, the Naval commander on the Dieppe raid; Captain 'Bloody' Pugsley RN and Commander 'Monkey' Sellar, the commanders of the Support Squadrons of Gun and Flak craft that had protected the Eastern Flank of the invasion beaches and later made the bloody assault on Walcheren Island; and Commander 'Red' Ryder who had won his V.C. for his part in the raid on St. Nazaire and who later commanded a Naval Intelligence Commando originated by Ian Fleming, the inventor of James Bond; or Commander 'Smokey' Prior, the Beachmaster, who, after the Dieppe raid escaped captivity and returned home via Paris and the Pyrenees to become Pugsley's Senior Staff Officer at Lepe; and Lieutenant Arthur Cheney RNVR who survived the destruction of his landing craft at Dieppe and at Walcheren Island, three times winner of the Distinguished Service Cross. Or the officers and seventy men of that fantastic, unique mini-monitor, LCF 1, with its two twin 4 inch destroyer gun mountings, veteran of Dieppe, blown to glory in a spectacular explosion in its magazines after being hit by an explosive German motor boat off the beaches of Normandy.

I went back to Exbury Gardens many times in the ensuing years and saw many changes as wartime structures were demolished and the gardens rearranged until there was no trace of the war. Eventually I could walk through the gardens for the sake of their beauty and fragrance, and not for sentiments of the past.

In November 1991 I heard, I forget how, that Mr. Edmund de Rothschild was organising a 50th anniversary reunion for former personnel of HMS Mastodon. I offered to help and became heavily involved. While reading the letters of those who applied for tickets for the event I became aware of how very little I knew about Mastodon, even though I had been based there for months during the autumn and winter of 1944/5. I asked the organisers to let me try to piece together the wartime history of Mastodon, or as much of it as I could before the reunion on 7th May 1992.

5. Mr. Edmund de Rothschild (left) and former Wren Jean Watson, planting a tree of remembrance at the HMS Mastodon re-union 1992

And I discovered that Exbury House was the centre of a number of famous places along the Beaulieu river collectively known as HMS Mastodon. They included the Master Builder's House hotel and Buckler's Hard where Nelson's warships had been designed and built. Also Bailey's Hard further upstream, the site of an even older shipyard now resuscitated to meet a new need. Also included were the Montagu Arms hotel at Beaulieu, Gilbury House at Exbury and Lepe House at the mouth of the Beaulieu river. I also discovered that there had been much more happening on the Beaulieu river, and along its banks, than was apparent from the existence of a naval base.

On both sides of the river, Special Operations Executive, SOE, had commandeered property for the training of agents and for hiding a troop of an extremely secret and little known unit of SOE Commandos. On the west bank, secret civil engineering projects had taken place and on the river itself there had been secret experiments with a fantastic pilotless, rocket-driven aircraft, a primitive forerunner of Cruise missiles. Also, moored in the river, there had been a number of Motor Torpedo Boats that had carried out secret hydrographic and agent-running missions.

HMS Mastodon existed for not much more than two and a half years but they were the momentous years of the second world war when the Allies were on the offensive in Europe, in the Mediterranean and in the Pacific war zones. By the time Mastodon was in its heyday, in the run-up to D-Day, the Allies had become expert in amphibious assaults and had devised all kinds of new techniques, gadgets and weaponry, some of it, I was to discover, developed on the Beaulieu river.

Before Exbury House became known as HMS Mastodon the primitive landing craft and weaponry of the infant Combined Operations organisation had lain in the lower reaches of the Beaulieu river prior to the fateful raid on Dieppe.

That debacle haunted Lord Louis Moutbatten, who had become Chief of Combined Operations, but he always maintained that it was necessary in order to learn the techniques and problems of amphibious assaults.

Learn we did from that disaster and by 1944 Combined Operations, or at least, the Naval component of it, was a complex organisation with a multiplicity of specialised

6. Remains of Beetles on the river bank of Southampton Water

units. Most of these units were represented at Mastodon which was a small scale representation of the whole of the Combined Operations organisation. I have managed to trace what happened to many of these units when they went overseas to do battle with the enemy, including the role played by the bits of the Mulberry harbour that were built on the west bank of the Beaulieu river. Some of these bits still exist along the riverbank of Southampton Water, at Dibden Bay.

Many of those who took an active part in these momentous eventful years are either dead or are in their seventies and eighties now, and soon their deeds will be forgotten if the memories of those who survive are not captured and recorded.

Of course, a great deal has been written about D-Day and of many of the Navy, Army and Air Force units that took part in it. There are several books that record

Hampshire's part in this period of history, but each deals with different bits of the story. I have tried to bring the relevant parts of these together and hopefully have added to them from a variety of sources, including letters from former naval personnel who served at Mastodon, and official documents in the Public Records Office, and in the D-Day and Royal Marines Museums. I have also obtained a wealth of information from a number of books and journals, almost all of them out of print, but which are held by the Maritime Section of the Portsmouth City Library.

CHAPTER 2
TWILIGHT WAR

When war was declared on 3rd September 1939 it was not exactly unexpected. Poland had been mercilessly attacked by Germany on September 1st. Within an hour or so of the announcement on our radios that war had been declared, air raid sirens sounded all over the country. A few people ran to the air raid shelters but most people stood in the streets and in the fields staring skywards expecting to see German aeroplanes and what they looked like, and wondering what it felt like to be bombed, as Warsaw had just been bombed and destroyed by the Luftwaffe's air armadas.

After staring into the empty sky for half an hour people went home and nothing happened for many months. They began to call it the phoney war, or, as Winston Churchill called it, Twilight War, a period of frantic preparation but little else for civilians to see, unless they were conscripted for military service.

Along the banks of the Beaulieu river and on the river itself little happened to disturb the tranquility. The river was cleared of all the pleasure craft and a few Nissen huts, corrugated iron arches on concrete bases with brick or wooden ends, appeared on the west bank.

On the east bank stood a number of mansions and large houses and estates, a few of which eventually played a part in the war. At the head of the river, six and a half miles from the Solent stands Palace House, the ancestral home of Lord Montagu. Two miles downstream lies Gilbury House, close to Gilbury hard and pier. Half a mile away, and inland, is Exbury House, one of the homes of the Rothschild family, with easy access to Gilbury Hard and pier. At the mouth of the Beaulieu river lies Inchmery House, a former residence of the Rothschild's before they bought Exbury. A mile to the east, facing the open water of the Solent stands Lepe House, once a smuggler's inn but

7. Gilbury pier as it is today

enlarged and modernised at the beginning of the present century to provide a home for Lord Forster, a former Tory M.P. and member of the Army Council and a former Governor General of Australia. His wife was the sister of the present Lord Montagu's father.

On the west bank of the river, about a mile downstream from Beaulieu, hidden among the trees, is Bailey's Hard, now barely recognisable as such but once the site of a 17th century shipyard. Nearby was a brickyard. One of the kilns is still there, intact.

Two snaking miles downstream, on the west bank and in a U bend of the river, lies Buckler's Hard, the famous shipyard that constructed Nelson's warships. It is far bigger in size than the minute Bailey's Hard but nevertheless its facilities are small and modest compared with shipyards capable of constructing modern ocean going warships of the size used during the second world war.

Downstream from Buckler's Hard hidden behind the trees and numerous creeks and inlets, there are several large houses and farms, served by a few, narrow roads. This side of the river is very rural and isolated, ideal for concealing secret units and activities from the public gaze.

8. Bailey's Hard

For most of its length the river banks are low and fringed with extensive mud flats, but on the west bank at Clobb Copse the mud and the river bank had been scooped out at the end of the last century to form oyster beds, creating a tidal basin about the size of a football pitch, parallel to and a few yards inshore of the river. It was to be used later in the war for unusual purposes by civil engineers.

The fairway of the river is narrow and shallow. Off Buckler's Hard there is barely nine feet of water on a low spring tide and the river remains this shallow almost down to its estuary, which, save for a narrow channel, is blocked off by the Warren Flat and Beaulieu Spit mudbanks at Needs Oar Point. The severe limitations that this places on its use by vessels of any kind needs no emphasis. Shipping movement is strictly regulated by the state and phase of the tides.

But events were to show that the Beaulieu river was just about deep enough to moor a type of warship that had not been invented in 1939. Also, it was ideal for use by barges and a new design of small troop-carrying craft that had just been invented but which had not yet proved its seaworthiness and value until used in the evacuation of beleaguered troops from the beaches of Dunkirk.

The Twilight War ended on 10th May 1940 when the Germans attacked Holland and Belgium and within sixteen days routed the French and British armies in France. On 26th May the Royal Navy began Operation Dynamo, the evacuation of troops from the beaches of Dunkirk. Admiral Sir Bertram Ramsey, who, four years later was to be the Commander of Naval Forces for the Allied invasion of Normandy, was in charge of the evacuation and used almost anything that would float, including motor yachts manned by civilian volunteers and paddle steamers, to bring the troops off the beaches.

Among the miscellany of small craft employed were eight of a brand new design of assault landing craft, (LCAs), and one Landing Craft Mechanised, (LCM). The LCAs were open launches, 39 feet long, 10 feet wide,

9. Oyster beds at Clobb Copse. The bollard on the left marks the entrance to the Floating Dock basin

7

driven by two Ford engines, ramped at the bows and weighing about ten tons so that they could be hoisted into ships' lifeboat davits. The LCM was a little longer and wider, had twice the weight and was propelled by water jets.

The LCAs were carried to Dunkirk in the davits of a cargo ship, the Clan Macalister, to do ship to shore work, and when the German shelling and bombing became too dangerous for the ship to remain off the beaches, it retreated and left the LCAs to find their own ways back to this country. They arrived days later, loaded with survivors at Margate, Ramsgate and Littlehampton.

The LCM was scuttled in mid-Channel when the skipper of the paddle steamer that was towing it became fed up with doing so!

The time was to come when updated versions of these little craft would be swarming into the Beaulieu river and routinely sent to sea in all weathers on navigation exercises to train their cox'ns and crews to hit the right beaches and find their ways back to their mother ships moored perhaps twenty miles away.

Even in defeat the new Prime Minister, Winston Churchill, was thinking of returning to the offensive and on 17th July 1940 the Combined Operations organisation was born and placed under the command of a 67 year old Admiral of the Fleet Sir Roger Keyes, who had made his name in similar operations in the first world war. The new organisation set up several bases, most of them in Scotland, but two were established in the Solent area, HMS Northney on Hayling Island, and HMS Tormentor in the Household Brigade's Yacht Club on the river Hamble.

At the same time orders were placed for the construction of 30 Tank Landing Craft, (TLCs), 152 feet long and 32 feet in the beam. When the first pair came into commission in November of the same year, they proved to be brutes to handle and almost impossible to steer, and they were declared unseaworthy! In the meantime, barges would have to suffice.

During the winter of 1940 Southampton was heavily bombed by the Luftwaffe and Husbands the shipbuilders was bombed out. To lessen the risk of a repetition, Husbands, at the suggestion of Captain The Honourable Pleydell-Bouverie, (who, in 1936, married the widow of John, Lord Montagu of Beaulieu), reopened the ancient

10. J Class Acoustic Minesweeper of the type fitted out by Husbands' at Bailey's Hard

shipyard at Bailey's Hard and on 11th March 1941 began fitting out small inshore minesweepers under the cover of the overhanging trees which acted as excellent camouflage. Ultimately eleven J Class minesweepers were completed here.

At about this time, or maybe a few months before, a small contingent of Naval personnel arrived on the west bank of the Beaulieu river and were accommodated in the Nissen huts that had been constructed at Bailey's and Buckler's Hards. Their presence presaged the arrival of no less than one hundred empty 'dumb' barges that were towed in convoys into the river booming like thunder as they banged together in the wind and tide.

Some planner with incredible foresight had decided to conserve a large supply of barges, or Thames lighters as they are often called. Designated 100, 150 and 200 ton types, and built principally of steel, they had capacious holds ten to fourteen feet deep and were blunt ended, flat bottomed and designed to sit on the artificial mud sills that adorned the front of just about every wharf in the Pool of London. They were very difficult to handle, except by experienced lightermen who, in the days of peace could be seen manoeuvring them, fully laden and decks awash, in the fast Thames tideway, using a single huge oar with consummate skill.

But the Naval party assigned to moor them on both sides of the Beaulieu river between Bailey's and Buckler's Hards were not, apparently, experienced lightermen. They had great difficulty mooring them, nose to the river banks, with heavy steel hawsers using the trees as bollards, and in tucking them into every available inlet and creek or on the mud flats.

One can only speculate as to where the barges came from. The most likely explanation is that they were cleared out of south coast ports to save them from devastating German air raids.

The barges lay in the river for almost eighteen months before the Naval shipwrights began a lengthy programme of fitting them with engines and cutting away one end and replacing it with a ramp that could be lowered to take a single vehicle. In other words converting them into landing barges or LBV's.

At the outbreak of war, the Navy had requisitioned the Puckpool holiday camp at Ryde on the Isle of Wight and renamed it HMS Medina. It became the main training and accommodation base for barge crews.

Ultimately the 100 barges, nearly a quarter of all the barges used in the Invasion, were pooled with 324 others from elsewhere that had been converted for all sorts of uses, including floating kitchens. They all did splendid service off Normandy and, later in the war, in the shallow waters and rivers of north west Europe.

Later in the war another type of barge, called Minca barges, were constructed on the Beaulieu river. They were made of wood, prefabricated in Canada and shipped in pieces to Liverpool. They were brought by rail to Beaulieu Road Station, and thence by road to either Buckler's Hard or Clobb Copse where they were assembled. There is no record of them having been used by the Ferry Units. They are not listed in the Navy's Green List of landing craft and barges, or mentioned anywhere in the Neptune Operation Orders. It is therefore probable that they were sent to south coast ports to replace the barges that had been requisitioned and converted into landing barges.

The year 1941 saw few other changes to disturb the Beaulieu river. But elsewhere the infant Combined Operations organisation was busily engaged in overseeing the construction of specialised landing ships and craft, training their crews and assault troops and planning operations in Europe, in the Mediterranean and off the east and west coasts of Africa. Most of these operations never took place and of those that did few were successful; some were a shambles.

At the end of 1941, Churchill became tired of what he scathingly described as Combined Operations 'pinpricks', and Sir Roger Keyes was replaced by Lord Louis Mountbatten, who had to relinquish command of an aircraft carrier to take up his new appointment.

*11. Earl Mountbatten,
Chief of Combined Operations*

On 7th December 1941, the Japanese attacked Pearl Harbour, America came into the war with her seemingly unlimited resources and began mass producing landing ships and craft, most of which had been designed by or in conjunction with the British Royal Corps of Naval Constructors. From here on, most of the tank landing ships, called LST's, and a huge number of minor landing craft, were manufactured in America. Most of the tank landing craft, the LCTs, and all the heavily armed variants of these hulls were built in Britain, mass produced by engineering firms, particularly bridge building firms, and not by conventional shipbuilders.

In the spring of 1942, Combined Operations was again reorganised, upgraded and began expanding rapidly. War came at last to the Beaulieu river but it was to be a temporary surge of activity lasting only a few months before subsiding.

On 13th April the river was requisitioned by the Admiralty and all the yacht moorings were cleared and replaced with heavy duty moorings and buoys laid in a fairly straight stretch of the river from Gilbury Hard downstream for just over a mile, to Gins Quay.

On the east bank of the river, Inchmery House had been requisitioned early in the war for use by the Free French Forces who had been rescued from the beaches of Dunkirk or had come to this country from elsewhere.

On 7th May 1942, Gilbury House, hard and pier, and Exbury House and the estate were requisitioned by the Navy. At the outbreak of the war, Mr. Lionel de Rothschild had offered Exbury House and the estate to the nation for use for war purposes, but the offer had not been taken up and the family continued to reside there. Now, at 48 hours notice, the Rothschild family had to move out. A coachload of naval ratings arrived to help them remove and store their possessions. During the move the naval ratings lived in the House and briefly enjoyed the comfort of the furnishings and fittings before these were removed and stored. They were replaced by the spartan standard Service iron bedsteads and double bunks, plywood furniture, coconut matting and Service mess traps. The naval ratings were turned out of the House and sent to the stable block to convert it into a habitable dormitory.

12. Mark 2 TLC of the type used at Dieppe

Within months the House was to be renamed HMS Mastodon, (all landing craft bases were named after pre-historic monsters and the irony was very apt), and turned into offices, storerooms and messes for officers and ratings. On the upper floor a sick bay was established under the supervision of two doctors, Surgeon Lieutenant V.C.Hassan and a colleague whose name is believed to be Henbury. There was also a Sick Berth Attendant, Allan Green. They were all attached to 'A' Squadron of Tank Landing Craft, TLCs, which was beginning to assemble in the Beaulieu river. Green remained at Exbury for the rest of the war and recalls that the first commanding officer of Exbury House was a Canadian, Lieutenant Commander Macglashen.

Within days another draft of naval ratings arrived, a contingent of 30 communications ratings, No.3 Beach Signals Section, which spent two weeks practising signalling on the roof of the House before moving on.

Soon after the heavy duty moorings had been laid in the river, the first tank landing craft arrived. They were twelve Mark 2s, slightly modified versions of the condemned and unwieldy Mark 1s, with an unloaded displacement of 300 tons but still only capable of carrying three heavy army tanks. They were propelled by three aero engines driving three screws, all turning the same way to make ship handling more of a misery than it was already. The engines required aviation fuel, two thousand gallons of high octane petrol, an additional hazard.

This was No.2 TLC Flotilla, the flotilla that was to bear the brunt of the casualties at Dieppe, and burn so fiercely when they were hit by enemy shells. It was to become the major part of 'A' Squadron under the command of David, the second Earl Beatty, the son of the famous World War 1 Admiral.

Earl Beatty had been the M.P. for Peckham, London, before being recalled to the Navy at the outbreak of the war, at the age of thirty four. After a couple of years in General Service, he was posted to Combined Operations, in February 1942. Now a Lieutenant Commander RN and working from Exbury House, it was his misfortune to be saddled with two new and untried types of vessels manned mostly by poorly trained and untried crews, and he had to train them for a beach assault on a heavily defended part of the French coast.

'A' Squadron was joined by another flotilla from the

13. Earl Beatty beckonong vehicles ashore

landing craft training base HMS Dinosaur at Troon. It was No.4 Flotilla, eqipped with twelve craft of a new and more seaworthy design, the Mark 3, thirty two feet longer, and heavier, than the Mark 2s, driven by two diesel engines and capable of lifting five heavy tanks. One of the commanding officers of these new craft was Peter Bull, a stage and film actor, who has written a graphic description of the difficulties he experienced manoeuvering his craft on and off the saltings to reach the trots. The Mark 3 craft were apparently too big and heavy to be manoeuvered between the marshes on either side of the Beaulieu river by their very inexperienced commanding officers and after one night in the river they moved round to Southampton, to 49 berth.

No.4 Flotilla was part of 'B' Squadron, also earmarked for the raid on Dieppe, under the command of Lieutenant Commander H. Mulleneux, RN, who was to lead them into battle after working them up in the Solent.

The Dieppe raid had been conceived in April, approved by the Chiefs of Staff in May and was due to take place on the first favourable day after 24th June. But training for the raid did not begin in earnest until the beginning of June when the British and Canadian troops began a series of exercises with the landing ships and craft in the Solent area, much of it on the shores of the Isle of Wight.

Earl Beatty's TLCs were joined by a new breed of uniquely British craft later to be called Support Craft. In June 1942, two of the Mark 2 TLC hulls then under construction in the north of England, had their tank holds decked over to carry anti-aircraft guns. Originally called Beach Patrol Craft or BPC's, their job was to provide inshore anti-aircraft cover for the beached TLCs.

The very first of these conversions, BPC No.1, (later misleadingly renamed Landing Craft Flak or LCF 1), was a unique and most remarkable craft, a mini-monitor. No other craft like her was ever built. Originally built as an experiment to see if the Mark 2 hull could withstand the stresses of heavy guns firing from her deck, she had a displacement of over 500 tons and was fitted with two twin 4 inch destroyer gun mountings and three 20mm Oerlikon guns. She was also given a bit of a bow instead of the usual flat front ramp welded to the hull. By the time she joined the force assembling for the Dieppe raid,

14. Mark 3 LCT

she had already battled with and sunk a German E boat, despite her slow speed and she was capable of fighting warships many times her size, being much more heavily armed than a wartime frigate.

She became the prototype for a new class of Support Craft, the Landing Craft Gun (Large) or LCG(L), but all subsequent vessels of this type carried only two 4.7 inch guns in single gun mountings, one mounted in front of the other.

The second conversion was less spectacular but was also destined to become the prototype of a new class of Support craft, the Landing Craft Flak, or LCF. Beach Patrol Craft No.2 had a displacement of about 500 tons and was also fitted with a deck over her tank space, upon which was mounted six two-pounder pom-poms (so called because of the rhythmic noise they made when fired) and four 20mm Oerlikon guns. She also had two more pom-poms mounted on platforms on either side of her flag deck, abaft the bridge. All subsequent LCFs were based on this pattern.

Both of these new designs were uniquely British; the Americans did not appreciate the need for inshore fighting vessels until the debacle at Omaha beach during the Invasion, after which they built similar craft based on Infantry Landing Craft (i.e., LCI(L)) hulls for the Pacific war zone.

BPCs 1 and 2 were unique in another respect; they were manned entirely by Navy crews of about 70 officers and ratings. In all later versions of these types of craft, the guns were manned by Royal Marines under a Royal Marines gunnery officer.

BPC 1 was allocated to 'B' Squadron assembling in Southampton Water. The ill-fated BPC 2 was allocated to Beatty's 'A' Squadron and moored in the Beaulieu river where she was later joined by BPCs 4 and 6. Two more BPCs, 3 and 5, joined the force at the very last minute. BPCs 3, 4, 5, and 6 were all replicas of BPC 2 and all were subsequently renamed Landing Craft Flak.

All the tank landing craft were sailing out of the Beaulieu river and Southampton to practice ship handling, navigation, beaching and loading in Osborne Bay and Egypt Point, just west of Cowes, where there are ferocious tides and currents. The troops had to practice backing their tanks and vehicles on to the landing craft and getting them off again across a variety of beach surfaces.

15. LCF 1 (originally BPC 1)

As the day for the assault approached, there was hectic activity at Exbury House, not only among the planners and Flotilla staffs but also among a team of shipwrights, hurriedly making collapsible dummy funnels and superstructures out of wood and canvas for each of the TLCs. One by one they came to Gilbury Hard to be fitted out. At the same time the craft had their original numbers painted out and were renumbered consecutively with the numbers 1 to 10.

When, ultimately, the assault convoy sailed from Newhaven, all the landing ships and craft left disguised as merchant ships. The landing craft sported an extra funnel and superstructure over their tank decks. The camouflage was removed during the night preceding the assault.

The Naval Force Commander who was ultimately

appointed to command the raid was Earl Mountbatten's Chief Naval Planner, Captain (later Commodore) J.Hughes-Hallett RN, a 41 year old Scot with aquiline features who was one of the founding fathers of Combined Operations. According to Mountbatten, went so badly that the raid was put back to the 8th July to allow for more training. On 7th July the force assembled in bad weather off Yarmouth, Isle of Wight. Suddenly four German bombers appeared and bombed the convoy, hitting two of the troop-carrying landing ships, (LSIs).

16. A typical Landing Craft Flak. This is one that moored in the Beaulieu River.

'Jock' Hughes-Hallett was very keen to discover what it was like for soldiers to make a seaborne assault landing, and he also wanted to find out about the competence and the morale of the Canadian troops who had been chosen to carry out the raid. For this purpose he was dressed in the uniform of a private soldier, given a few lessons in soldiering and was then posted to the Canadian Camerons Regiment in their tented camp at Wooton Creek in the Isle of Wight. He participated in two rehearsals and was with the Canadians, still in disguise, when they were told their destination and were briefed for the raid. Afterwards he returned to London to report that the Canadians were 'wildly enthusiastic'. He also had a fund of stories about what it was like to be a comparatively elderly and inefficient private soldier among a platoon of keen young soldiers.

In mid-June a final rehearsal took place at West Bay, and

The operation was cancelled and the ships and men dispersed. Which was very fortunate because the Germans had read their tide tables and watched the force assembling and were prepared and waiting for the assault.

The two TLC flotillas and the six BPCs returned to their moorings in the Beaulieu river and Southampton.

The Dieppe raid, Operation Jubilee, eventually took place in the early morning of 19th August, with Hughes-Hallett directing the assault from the destroyer HMS Calpe. An hour before the landing the assault convoy had the misfortune to run into a German merchant convoy and its armed escorts. In the ensuing melee BPC 1, which was carrying assault troops including U.S. Rangers, was hit by enemy shellfire, and her commanding officer and many of the troops were wounded, but she kept on firing her four 4 inch guns at enemy shipping, shore targets and aircraft.

BPC 2 received a direct hit with a bomb and sank within minutes, with heavy loss of life, after an operational life of barely two months.

No.2 TLC Flotilla was annihilated. After managing to land all but one of their tanks on the beaches, two craft

17. Landing Craft and tanks burning on the beach at Dieppe

No.s 121 & 145 were destroyed on the beaches. Three No.s 124,126 & 159 sank offshore and the other five were badly damaged. Every one of the tanks that they had put ashore at great cost to themselves were destroyed, most before they could leave the beaches.

Lieutenant Arthur Cheney RNVR, the commanding officer of TLC 126, was rescued, wounded, after beaching twice under heavy shellfire to offload his vehicles and commandos. His craft was hit in the engine room and was on fire. It sank as he left the beach on the second occasion. He was subsequently awarded the Distinguished Service Cross. Later in the war he earned two bars to his DSC as the commanding officer of Support craft. He had numerous miraculous escapes from death and became one of the heroes of the Naval Support Squadrons. After subsequent service in the Mediterranean, he returned to home waters and was to anchor his Gun Craft in the Beaulieu river and visit Mastodon (Exbury House) on a number of occasions before the war in Europe ended.

The Dieppe raid produced about 4,600 casualties in killed, wounded, missing and made prisoners of war. The Navy suffered 550 casualties. The raiding force retreated to Newhaven from where the 4th TLC Flotilla, which had remained well offshore and had not beached during the raid, sailed to Stokes Bay to unload their troops and cargoes before returning to their berths in Southampton and 48 hours well earned leave.

A great deal has been written about the Dieppe raid but one thing that has never been said is that it put an end to the wildcatting with assault techniques and to the amateurism that had blighted many Combined Operations.

The raid made it painfully obvious that a frontal assault on a defended port was impractical and it was never tried again. Combined Operations learned some nasty lessons which set off a train of inventions and the raising of new units and craft specialising in various aspects of assaults, two of which are relevant here. After the raid, Captain J.Hughes-Hallett, the Naval Force Commander remarked, "Well, if we can't capture a port intact we will have to take one with us." The other was the obvious need for an inshore craft capable of drenching the beaches with explosives before an assault was attempted. Hughes-Hallett's remark gave birth to the Mulberry Harbour; the second need gave birth to the LCT(R), a tank landing craft converted to fire 1080 heavy rockets in ripple salvos.

After the raid, all that remained of No.2 Flotilla, in the Beaulieu river was TLC 128, which had not gone on the raid. She was joined at her moorings by No.5 Flotilla, a brand new design of tank landing craft, or LCTs as they were now known, the Mark 4, which had a loaded displacement of 586 tons, was twenty seven feet longer and eight feet wider than 128, a Mark 2, and, surprisingly, shallower in draught by two and a half feet, which is very surprising in view of her displacement, and significant in view of the shallowness of the river.

No.5 Flotilla, which had been anchored off Calshot during the raid, replaced the annihilated No.2 Flotilla under Earl Beatty's command, together with the remains of his Support Flotilla, LCFs 4 and 6.

Exbury House remained the HQ of 'A' Squadron, which in the ensuing months was reinforced by another LCT flotilla, the 21st, and by the addition of LCFs 1, 3 and 5. LCF 5 had acted as the hospital craft during the raid and had shot down five enemy aircraft. Most of these craft were berthed in Southampton, leaving the Beaulieu river moorings almost empty except for occasional visiting craft, although the 100 dumb barges still lined the shores.

In December, Earl Beatty and his 'A' Squadron staff and craft moved to Southampton, and HMS Mastodon all but died, except for the barges being converted into LBV's.

CHAPTER 3
INNOVATION AND EXPERIMENTATION

There were several reasons for the near demise of Exbury as a landing craft base. The Mediterranean was about to become the principal theatre of war for Combined Operations. Three months after the Dieppe raid, in November 1942, the Allies landed in force on the north west coast of Africa, on the shores of Morocco and Algeria. It was called Operation Torch. Another huge landing, called Operation Husky, was planned for July 1943 on the coast of Sicily. It was already draining off resources of tank landing craft, the new Flak and Gun craft and the new American-built Infantry Landing Craft, the LCI(L)s, designed in Britain at Churchill's request for a 'giant raiding craft' and manned by British crews who had sailed them direct from the American shipyards to the Mediterranean.

Another reason for the run-down of Exbury was that the Force created for the Dieppe raid, called J Force, (not to be confused with another J Force created for D-Day), was being plundered of ships and craft for other purposes. It had been commanded by Captain J.Hughes-Hallett RN who had taken over the Royal Yacht Squadron premises at Cowes, renamed HMS Vectis, as his headquarters.

In May 1943, the old J Force virtually ceased to exist. The officer complememnt was cut to the bone and so was that of HMS Squid at Southampton, which was reduced to two officers on its staff. Exbury was left with one and his name was Lieutenant Commander H.S.Robinson RNVR, who was in charge of HMS Mastodon.

There is some doubt as to when Exbury House was officially commissioned as HMS Mastodon. The earliest people who served there knew it only as Exbury House

18. Landing Barge Vehicle of the type converted on the Beaulieu River

and the name Mastodon does not appear in the Navy List until February 1943, although Robinson is known to have taken up his appointment in December 1942.

At about this time Mastodon had on its books, but not at its moorings, the 4th, 5th and 21st LCT Flotillas and the remnants of the 1st LCF Flotilla. Both the 4th and the 21st Flotillas were destined for the Mediterranean theatre, along with Flak craft 4 and 5, and they had all gone by March. Thereafter the Beaulieu river was only occasionally visited by a few major landing craft and some Motor Torpedo Boats. However the 100 barges still resided in the river but had significantly changed their status. By 5th January they had all been fitted with engines at one end and ramps at the other and were now being classed as LBV(M), i.e. Landing Barge Vehicle (Mechanised).

During the Christmas period of 1942 Robinson recruited a Wren secretary, Ena Smith. She lived locally but had been working at Fort Southwick on Portsdown Hill, near Portsmouth. She states that when she started working at Exbury the small number of naval ratings already there were mainly survivors of ships that had been sunk or damaged by enemy action. For them it was a convalescent posting.

Life appears to have been very pleasant and very casual. Ena Smith called this period the 'phoney war'; there was little for anybody to do and she had plenty of time to enjoy walking in the beautiful gardens which were still being maintained by the Rothschild's gardeners, and she played a lot of tennis, often with Robinson.

Across the river at Buckler's Hard there was another lone Wren, Barbara Spreadbury, who many years later was to become the mayor of Christchurch on a number of occasions. She was the only woman among 40 'bargees', that is, ratings from HMS Medina who were learning to crew the barges and who were quartered in the Nissen huts at Buckler's and Bailey's Hards. Occasionally Wren Spreadbury was brought across the river to Exbury for a little female company with Ena Smith. This casual existence continued for many months.

Although little was happening at Exbury, 1942 and 1943 were years of intense planning for the invasion of France and of much experimentation and weapon and craft development.

In 1942, Wates, the building construction company, in conjunction with Marley Ltd., the well known tile manufacturing company, began experimenting with the construction of vessels in concrete at Clobb Copse. Marley's had years of experience in using concrete for manufacturing a variety of building products, from floor and roofing tiles to small prefabricated buildings. The choice of Clobb Copse oyster beds as the site for the experiments was due largely to the peacetime yachting interests of Mr. Owen (later Sir Owen) Aisher, the head of Marley's. He was a keen yachtsman, knew the Beaulieu river well and had recognised the construction potential of the oyster beds.

During 1943 a basin was dredged out of the mud adjacent to the oyster beds and a hundred men were employed on the construction of a large floating dock out of concrete. It was launched in April 1944. It was probably the largest vessel ever to have been floated out

19. Floating Dock basin at Clobb Copse

into the Beaulieu river and was towed away over the period of two tides, piloted from a rowing boat by Frank Downer, Beaulieu's redoubtable Harbour Master, pulling ahead of the tug. It was large enough to take a 'Flower' class corvette, or a tank landing craft which was the same size. It was towed to Ceylon. After the war it was towed back to Europe and it is still in use to this day, in Norway.

The Dieppe raid had demonstrated only too clearly that the Germans would fight tenaciously to prevent the Allies from capturing a port, or, if they did, it would certainly be left in ruins. And without a port the Allies would not be able to shift sufficient supplies to support their invading armies.

Hughes-Hallet's idea of making a portable port and towing it across the English Channel behind the invading armies seemed ludicrous, but that is what was ultimately achieved. Indeed not one, but two ports each a little larger than Dover were constructed, one for the American sector, the other for the British sector. Both were towed in pieces across to Normandy and both were given the same code name, 'Mulberry'.

The idea was not finally 'sold' to the Service Chiefs by Lord Louis Mountbatten until 5th August 1943, while they were crossing the Atlantic in the Cunard liner Queen Mary. However, months before that date experiments had taken place into all sorts of problems associated with the project.

The principle problem was not so much concerned with the manufacture and construction of the port unloading facilities, piers and jetties as with protecting them from bad weather and heavy seas once they had been placed into position.

The construction problems associated with the port installations were given to the Army. The problems of defending them against the seas and of transporting all the pieces to France was given to the Navy.

The whole project was gigantic in scale and was to consume 630,000 tons of concrete and employ 15,000 workmen. The whole thing had to be designed, tested, modified and completed in eight months! Moreover, it had to be kept secret and concealed from the Germans.

Among the many local sites used for the construction of various pieces were the site of the old Marchwood power

20. The floating dock constructed at Clobb Copse

station, Lepe beach, at the mouth of the Beaulieu river, and the oyster beds at Clobb Copse. Responsibilities were allotted to the Services and the civil engineers on 3rd September 1943, but mass construction did not start until December.

size, the largest being 200 feet long, 50 feet wide and 60 feet high, all made of reinforced concrete and weighing 6,000 tons. They had to float like ships so that they could be towed across the Channel to their positions before being scuttled to rest firmly on the seabed. Each one took

21. Phoenix slipways on Lepe beach

There were three main types of structures for the Mulberry Harbour. The first was the construction of the long pierhead, capable of berthing and handling cargo vessels, landing ships and landing craft in substantial numbers. Associated with this was the construction of floating roadways running from the pierheads and subsidiary jetties to the beach. The roadways had to be very long to cope with the gentle gradient of the Normandy beaches and the rise and fall of the tides. Much of the metalwork for the pierheads and roadways was assembled at Marchwood.

The second part of the structure was the three-mile long breakwater, spread to seaward and at each side of the port facilities to create an enclosed harbour. It had two components, old cargo vessels and warships that were to be scuttled, and immense concrete structures that were given the code name 'Phoenix'. These varied in

over a month to build by a small army of carpenters and labourers. Each had internal chambers for accommodating the soldiers working the port and also anti-aircraft gun crews, and they were all fitted with massive pumps so that they could be sunk or raised at will. Over 200 of these structures were needed for the harbour.

About six of them were built by 700 men on the foreshore at Lepe, and as each one was completed it was launched sideways into the Solent down six narrow concrete slipways which are still to be seen running into the water at Stansore Point.

The third element, which is rarely mentioned, was a hugh device to break the force of the waves before they reached the harbour walls. Code named 'Bombardon', they were made of steel and were girder-like contraptions 200 feet long, 25 feet high and 25 feet wide,

22. Beetles under construction in the oyster beds at Clobb Copse.

built with a cruciform cross section. A long line of 115 of them was moored three miles to seaward of the harbour.

During the autumn of 1943, at Clobb Copse, on the west bank of the Beaulieu river, adjacent to where the floating dock was still under construction, the oyster beds themselves were dredged out by Wates and Marley to make a basin for constructing pieces required for supporting the floating roadway. The floats, i.e., the pontoons, called 'Beetles', were made almost entirely of concrete. They were 42 feet long, 15 feet wide and about

23. A completed Beetle being towed away

7 feet deep and looked like dumb lighters with a beetle-back concrete lid over their holds. They weighed many tons; the prototype weighed 87 tons. Four hundred and seventy of them were needed to support the roadways, of which upwards of fifty were produced in the oyster beds at Clobb Copse. They all had to be towed across the Channel behind all kinds of vessels including LCTs.

The remains of thirty of these Beetles are to be seen today propping up the riverbank of Southampton Water at Dibden Bay, between Hythe Marina and Husbands shipyard.

After the completion of the Beetle programme, a number of concrete dumb lighters were built by Wates and Marley. A few were seen moored off Clobb Copse during the winter of 1944. It is known that a small number of concrete lighters were used during the invasion.

The second type of unit produced in the mud basins in the banks of the river was very much larger than the Beetles. They were called Intermediate Pontoons, to be moored at the seaward end of the floating roadways adjacent to the pierheads. The tops of these concrete structures were 80 feet by 60 feet and they contained eighteen chambers, two of which were store rooms and a third was to be used for accommodation purposes. Six of these monsters were built in the river. On completion they were floated out of their basins by demolishing the retaining wall nearest to the river.

The construction of the floating dock and the Mulberry Harbour units required a considerable work force of labourers and carpenters who were bused in daily from the surrounding area. Also, substantial storage sheds were constructed, the foundations of which remain to this day in the shubbery of the garden of the house, now occupied by Sir Owen Aisher's son, also named Owen Aisher.

Nearby there were four houses, Clobb Gorse, The Drokes, Warren House, and The House by the Shore occupied by trainee agents of the Special Operations Executive. S.O.E. had requisitioned no fewer than eleven private houses in the vicinity of Beaulieu for their 'Finishing School' for trainee agents of many nationalities. Here they learned, among many other topics, how to avoid detection and resistance to interrogation.

24. S.O.E. headquarters The Rings, since demolished.

Contrary to local rumour, Palace House was never used as the S.O.E. headquarters. This was located in a house called The Rings, since demolished. Palace House was used as the local Air Raid Precautions (ARP) and Red Cross headquarters and was later earmarked as a stand-by headquarters for the Allied Supreme Commander, General Eisenhower.

Warren House near Needs Oar Point and The House by the Shore at Sowley, overlooking and the Solent, seem to have been used for training agents to fire a variety of weapons, including anti-tank weapons.

Three months before D-Day, an advance airfield was set up at Park Farm and was used by four squadrons of RAF Typhoon aircraft.

On the opposite bank, near the mouth of the river, Inchmery House had been requisitioned early in the war and became a commando training school for Polish and

French troops of the Free French Combat Parachute Company. The Poles used to play netball with the local girls in the playground of Exbury school. On completion of their commando training the parachutists were sent to North Africa where, in a series of daring raids against

25. Inchmery House, headquarters of the Free French B.C.R.A.

enemy airfields they sustained very heavy casualties. By 1942 Inchmery House was occupied by the Free French equivalent of S.O.E. which had the clumsy title of Bureau Central de Rensignements et Action, or BCRA. Bitter rivalry was to develop between the French Section of S.O.E. and De Gaulle's BCRA.

In October 1942 a troop of the Small Scale Raiding Force, the SSRF, was based at Inchmery and remained there until the Force was disbanded in April 1943.

The SSRF was also known as 62 Commando, perhaps the most secret of all the commando units that were raised during the war. There were only four troops of them in this country, manned by British, French and other Continental personnel, including, probably, a few Germans. They were commanded from a manor house near Bere Regis in Dorset by Lieutenant Colonel Bill Stirling, brother of David Stirling the founder of the S.A.S. During 1942 until they were disbanded they made countless small scale raids on the enemy coasts from Norway to the Spanish border, and also upon the Channel Islands. They were attached to S.O.E. for the purpose of securing small beachheads for the infiltration and evacuation of agents. They are believed to have ferried the agents from ship or submarine to shore and were also used to gather local intelligence and take German prisoners.

At the end of 1942 the SSRF came under the operational command of Captain J.Hughes-Hallett at Cowes, and while under his command made several raids on the French coast to gather intelligence related to the Invasion plans.

One can only speculate as to whether S.O.E., the BCRA and the SSRF used the Beaulieu river for their nefarious comings and goings. They frequently used Motor Torpedo Boats or Gun Boats to transport their agents and commandos. Some of the boats they used were also used by Combined Operations to take beach reconnaisance units across to France.

It is highly likely that some of the Coastal Forces craft seen lurking in the Beaulieu river at this time were engaged in transporting agents or commandos across to the Far Shore and for training them to launch dories and fol-boats, (collapsible canoes), paddle them ashore unseen and return and re-embark speedily and noiselessly.

One of the costliest lessons learned from the Dieppe raid was the need for inshore craft capable of demolishing enemy gun emplacements and saturating the beach defences with explosives. Shortly after the raid, Combined Operations Headquarters 'asked for trials to be carried out for fitting rocket projectors to landing craft', and on 27th November 1942 the Admiralty approved the conversion of LCT 161, to carry rockets. It was a Mark 2 hull and a sister craft of those annihilated at Dieppe.

The idea of the Rocket Craft, or LCT(R), is attributed to Colonel F.H.G.Langley, a member of the headquarters staff of Combined Operations. The task of developing the idea was passed to the Admiralty's Department of Miscellaneous Weapons Development, (DMWD) and to the Combined Operations Experimental Establishment at Appledore, at the estuary of the north Devon river Taw.

could be fired simultaneously without damaging or destroying the craft. It took place before 'a large and distinguished audience'. Many of the people there looked on with misgivings at the mass of rocket projectors pointing from the modified LCT 161, because tail-less

26. Rocket Craft, carrying 1080 heavy rockets

Both of these organisations were also involved with the problem of breaking the force of the waves before they reached the proposed Mulberry Harbour installations.

The head of an engineering section of DMWD, and also the leader of a team dealing with rocketry, was a stress engineer from the aircraft industry who was already a famous novelist. His name was Lieutenant Commander N.S.Norway RNVR, better known as Nevil Shute. Among his many wartime interests was experimenting with flamethrowers, drone aircraft, rockets and rocket-propelled devices, including a pilotless rocket aircraft. He took a major role in the design of the projectors for the Rocket Craft.

The first trial of the new LCT(R), the Rocket craft, took place in bad weather off Spithead, just outside Portsmouth Harbour, on 11th April 1943, and it was intended to answer the question of how many rockets

rockets had a nasty habit of going off in all directions. The observers from the Corps of Naval Constructors feared that the heat generated by so many rockets would blow up the whole vessel as the rockets were fired.

During the first trial the size of the salvos was increased until it reached 33 rockets, at which point six salvos were to be fired at half second intervals, launching 198 rockets altogether. But by the fourth salvo the searing heat was building up so fast that it endangered the lives of the two scientists aboard the craft. So violent was the back blast that the 560 ton vessel was making sternway as each salvo left the deck. One eyewitness stated that there was a shattering roar, sheets of flame and billowing smoke and afterwards the craft's White Ensign was in tatters and the two scientists emerged from the smoke devoid of eyebrows, with singed hair and clothing, and blackened faces. Many of the spectators thought that the craft had blown up and were surprised to see that it the was still there after the smoke had cleared.

At the second trial ten days later the rockets were fired by remote control, which was very fortunate because during the firing of 759 rockets in salvos of 33, an electrical fault led to two salvos firing simultaneously and caused the temperature to rise to 1,000 degrees, melting the bridge of the craft and destroying all the scientific instruments that had been carefully placed on board.

Subsequently the craft were fitted with a blast screen between the rocket projectors and the bridge and a blast proof booth was fitted to the deck for the commanding officers to crouch in during firings.

After the third trial on 28th April the Admiralty ordered 30 LCTs to be converted into Rocket Craft and six of them made their debut at the invasion of Sicily on 10th July 1943. The invention proved to be a winner.

The LCT(R) were manned by a crew of two officers and fifteen ratings. Each craft could fire 1080 heavy rockets in 26 seconds, sending 17 tons of explosives flying through the air for a considerable distance. It was said to be equivalent to 80 cruisers bombarding simultaneously. Yet despite its ingenuity, it was a one-shot weapon because it took hours to reload, and each craft carried only one reload. The awesome ferocity of its fire power could not conceal a system of gunnery not much better than Nelson's warships. The rocket projectors were all set at the same angle, pointing skywards at about 45 degrees off the perpendicular, and the craft itself, aided by its own radar, had to be aimed at the target area with great accuracy, despite wind and tide, the vagaries of steering the Mark 2 hulls and any distracting enemy bombing or shell fire. With such a primitive weapon there were, inevitably, accidents. Rockets occasionally fell short among our own troops and landing craft, with devastating effect and loss of life.

Despite all the fears voiced about the dangers of these craft blowing themselves up, or being blown up if hit by enemy bombs or shell fire, none blew up in action, even when hit; one was hit seven times during one action and survived. Ironically, ship casualty records reveal that they were the safest of all the major landing craft to serve in, safer even than the humble LCTs!

Two of the very first Rocket craft were moored in Southampton and went on many training exercises at Stokes Bay and did their rocket firing training at Studland Bay. They proved to be a very successful weapon wherever they were used and became a familiar sight in the Beaulieu river both before and after D-Day.

In April 1943 a team of over 20 soldiers with eight three-ton lorries arrived at Lepe and were billeted at Lepe House which was still a private residence. Over the next few days the men struggled with empty 40 gallon oil drums and metal air tanks and with fitting together three-inch metal poles until they had made a large floating contraption which was then dressed with a canvas superstructure. It was towed by the Navy down the west Solent but the tug broke down and the contraption began drifting out to sea before it could be rescued by another tug. It was towed back to Lepe, dismantled, loaded on to the lorries and driven away.

Three months later the Military Police arrived in force at the Master Builder's House hotel at Buckler's Hard and took over all the rooms overlooking the hard. They also insinuated themselves into adjacent cottages that had rooms overlooking the hard. Simultaneously, restrictions were placed on the movement of people in the area, Service and civilian.

On 6th July a team of 20 men of the Pioneer Corps unloaded eight three-ton lorries and after many hours of work assembling floating tanks, lengths of piping and rolls of canvas, they produced a full scale dummy Mark 2 tank landing craft. The Navy towed it down the river and moored it off Clobb Copse near to a real Mark 4 LCT. Overhead a circling RAF aircraft was taking photographs which, when developed, showed that the dummy appeared realistic, except that it was too clean, a defect that was later remedied with rust-coloured paint and old engine oil. The dummy was towed back to Buckler's Hard, dismantled and driven away with the Military Police.

The two brief appearances were the very first trials of prototype dummy LCTs, part of a deception plan known as Operation Quicksilver, the creation of a dummy landing craft fleet to act as a feint against the Pas de Calais.

Six weeks after the second trial, on 13th and 14th August, a large convoy of about 60 lorries containing heavy equipment and over 100 men of the Pioneer Corps again arrived at Buckler's Hard and under the cloak of darkness and with great secrecy took two nights to assemble seven dummy LCTs. The dummies were now known as Bigbobs.

The Navy forgot to send their tugs and there was some confusion and much delay while awaiting the arrival from Portsmouth of part of a flotilla of LCVPs, assault landing craft, manned by Royal Marines, to act as tugs. The LCVPs were the American Navy's equivalent of the Jeep; 23,358 of them were built. They were highly versatile 36 foot fast runabouts, ramped at the bow so that they could take either one vehicle of 36 men. They usually had a crew of three, two marines and a corporal-cox'n and were a very common sight all over the Solent area and in the Beaulieu river where they were used as trot boats, 'manned' by a Wren Petty Officer cox'n and two Wrens.

The LCVPs towed the seven Bigbobs down the river to the moorings off Clobb Copse and left them there until September when they were returned to Buckler's Hard, dismantled and driven away in a fleet of lorries,

By D-Day, almost a year later, 300 of these dummies had been manufactured. They were erected and moored along the east coast between Great Yarmouth and Folkstone to fool the Germans into believing that a huge awaiting army was preparing to invade France and the Low Countries across the Pas de Calais.

The Beaulieu river, which had already witnessed the prototypes of LCTs, and the Gun and Flak craft, and experimentation with concrete vessels for the Mulberry Harbour, had once again witnessed the trials of yet another new device.

CHAPTER 4
THE REFORMATION OF HMS MASTODON

On 3rd August 1943, Lord Louis Mountbatten's Combined Operations Headquarters presented their plans for the invasion of France to the Anglo-American Combined Chiefs of Staff. Code named Operation Overlord, the invasion was planned for June 1944 from five beachheads in the Baie de Seine on the coast of Normandy. The two western beachheads, code named Utah and Omaha, at the neck of the Cherbourg peninsula, were to be established by the American forces. The other three, called Gold, Juno and Sword, were to be established by the British and Canadian forces.

The colossal task of lifting the armies across the Channel to their respective beachheads, and supporting them when they landed, was placed in the hands of a British Admiral because the majority of the many thousands of vessels that would be involved were British. The commander of this naval armada was to be Admiral Sir Bertram Ramsey, the same man who three years previously had organised the evacuation of the British and Allied troops from the beaches of Dunkirk.

Admiral Ramsey eventually made his headquarters at Southwick House at the foot of the Portsdown Hills, just outside Portsmouth. He divided the British and Canadian assault forces into three commands according to the beaches they were going to assault, that is, G Force would assault the Gold sector, J Force the Juno sector and S Force the Sword sector. Each of the Forces was sub-divided into three Assault Groups and each Group was commanded by a naval Captain.

The operations headquarters for the three Force commanders was the premises of the Royal Yacht Squadron at Cowes, HMS Vectis, under Vice Admiral Moore, whose staff eventually grew to 56 Naval officers

27. Admiral Ramsey

and 16 WRNS officers. The first of the three Forces to be created was J Force, a title resuscitated from the Dieppe days and by accident or design containing many of the original landing ships and some of the landing craft of those days.

The new J Force was commanded by Commodore G.N.Oliver, RN, and one of his first Group commanders to be appointed was Captain A.F.Pugsley, RN. Pugsley was a destroyer man and had just relinquished command, somewhat reluctantly, of the destroyer HMS Jervis. He knew little about Combined Operations when he reported to Cowes, where he learned that he had been appointmented as the commander of Assault Group J.1. He seems to have been a thrusting, energetic man of forty three years of age and was eventually to rise to the rank of Rear Admiral after making a formidable reputation for himself, later in the war as the commander of the naval forces that made the bloody assault on Walcheren Island in the estuary of the Scheldt.

One of his first acts was to requisition Lepe House, the residence of Lady Forster, for his headquarters, in September 1943. Soon he had a staff of seven Naval

28. Captain A. F. Pugsley RN

officers, several WRNS officers, a large number of Wrens and just twelve naval ratings to guard the premises.

His Senior Staff Officer was Commander R.M.Prior, RN, an extraordinary man who acquired the nickname 'Smokey' because of his love of smoke screens to cover assaults from the sea. He was a former Member of Parliament and had been a Beachmaster during the Dieppe raid and had been left on the beach, wounded, when the raiding force withdrew. Somehow he evaded captivity and, still wearing his uniform and seaboots, which gave him the appearance of a fisherman, made his way to Paris from where pre-war friends smuggled him to the south of France, across the Pyrenees into Spain and thence back to this country. After D-Day he remained on Pugsley's staff and became a Beachmaster for the assault on Walcheren Island.

The Wrens at Lepe House were doing all the secretarial, communications and clerical work for J.1. Assault Group, and were also running the mess and wardroom for an increasing number of staff and visiting officers.

From this date onwards, there was a dramatic change in the fortunes of HMS Mastodon, which was given the job of administering the J Force headquarters at Lepe.

Within two months of Pugsley's appointment, the Navy requisitioned all the premises at Buckler's Hard, including the Master Builder's House hotel and drafted in a large number of men, a high proportion of whom were artificers, to set up a repair and maintenance base for major and minor landing craft.

The status of Mastodon was transformed. Lieutenant Commander Robinson was replaced by a regular naval officer, Commander R.K.C.Pope, DSO, OBE., who now became responsible for Exbury House, Gilbury House and Lepe House on the east bank of the Beaulieu river, and the Master Builder's House hotel, many of the cottages at Buckler's Hard and the Buckler's Hard facilities on the west bank.

Up to this point there had been very few Wrens at

29. Lepe House as it is today; the signal tower was on the top of the bay window on the right

Exbury, about fourteen of them altogether acting as mess stewards, clerks and telephone and teleprinter operators, and they had been accommodated in Exbury House. But in the autumn there had been a steady increase in their number in order to cope with the voracious demands of

30. The Montagu Arms during the war

Pugsley's headquarters as well as the increasing work loads placed on Mastodon itself. Before the end of the year there were about a hundred Wrens and their officers to be accommodated, and the Montagu Arms hotel in Beaulieu was requisitioned for this purpose.

The Wrens were now doing a wide range of duties besides stewarding, clerical, administrative, coding and communications work. Many were driving lorries, issuing supplies of all kinds, acting as mechanics in the transport pool, in the Buckler's Hard repair facility and in the trot boats. They were also providing trot boat crews to ferry personnel and supplies to the landing craft moored down the river, and to the new jetty and hard that was being built on the beach in front of Lepe House. The hard, officially designated Q Hard, could accommodate four tank landing craft at any one time, and the jetty had pipes for supplying them with fuel and fresh water from the large storage tanks that were being built in the garden of Lepe House.

The remains of Q Hard are still to be seen on the beach in front of Lepe House at low tide. The House itself acquired a signal tower on top of its bay windows, overlooking the entrance to the Beaulieu river, from where flag or Aldis lamp signals could be made to all craft entering or leaving the river.

The number of naval ratings arriving at Mastodon was also increasing rapidly until it reached a total of ninety. Until now, the number of temporary buildings disfiguring the grounds of Exbury House had been limited. Many of the new arrivals, including increasingly large contingents of communication ratings, had to be accommodated at first in bell tents, but as their number grew and with the rapid increase in the volume of stores required to support them and the landing craft arriving in the river, stores and men were being moved out of the House and tents into the huts that were being errected in the grounds to the south of the House. Eventually barracks capable of housing perhaps three hundred men, and supply sheds, a cinema and a sick bay and dental surgery were built around the house and to the south east of it, close to the road to Lower Exbury. A guard house was built just inside the old main entrance to the estate, behind the Lodge. A transport pool of three-ton lorries, pick-ups and cars was situated half way down and to the left of the main drive.

Between the spring and autumn of 1943 few landing craft had been moored in the river, but during this period the 100 dumb barges that had been converted into LBV's and fitted with ramps and engines were being regularly sailed away in batches to various south coast locations, many of them to Langstone harbour. By November there were only five left in the river and by Christmas they had all gone.

During the summer and early autumn increasing numbers of tank landing craft were arriving in the Solent and at Southampton from their training base at Troon. There was also a very rapid increase in the number of

29

LCVPs, the run-abouts, and the much larger Landing Craft Mechanised, LCMs, all of which moored at Calshot, in the sheltered water behind the Spit, and attached to the Calshot Naval Unit. It is believed that this Unit was administered from Mastodon.

the breakwater of the Mulberry Harbour.

The LCMs attached to the Calshot Naval Unit were often to be seen plying up and down the Beaulieu river and a whole Squadron of LCVPs, that is, sixty craft, was eventually to be based at Mastodon.

31. Mark 4 LCT alongside a jetty similar to the one at Lepe

The LCVPs, the LCMs and the barges, were all part of what were officially known as Ferry Units. Very little has been written about these units and the vital role they played during the build-up phase of the invasion. They transported men and materials from ship to shore, acted as trot boats and tugs and performed a wide variety of duties before and after the Mulberry Harbour became operational, under constant shell fire from enemy shore batteries. They have never been given the credit they deserve. All these craft were open boats with no crew accommodation. They were manned by naval ratings, Royal Marines or soldiers from the Royal Army Service Corps. The men lived rough in their craft for many weeks and had to collect their hot meals from barges that had been converted to floating kitchens. Some of the Ferry Unit crews eventually found shelter and accommodation in the superstructures above the waterline of the sunken block ships that formed part of

32. Kitchen Barge off the Normandy beaches capable of serving 900 hot meals a day

Around the end of the year, Mastodon was upgraded again. Commander Pope was replaced by a four-ring Captain by the name of Roland Swinley. Swinley was a tall, lean man with greying hair in his late forties. He had been a handsome man when he was younger. Before the war, he

33. LCM of the type based at Calshot

had been one of a band of dashing destroyer captains in the Mediterranean Fleet, renowned for their ship handling skills and for their heavy drinking. Swinley had a fearsome reputation due to his penchant for court-martialling his subordinate officers and for hounding them and his crews unmercifully. He was reputedly a Jekyll and Hyde character who could be as charming and thoughtful when he wished to be as he was thoughtless, ruthless and unforgiving to his subordinates and to anybody he disliked. He was a naval officer of the old school, an imperious autocrat. Before he was promoted to the rank of Captain to take command of Mastodon, he had been the Training Commander of the Coastal Forces working-up base, HMS Bee, at Weymouth.

Practically all Training Commanders in small ship bases everywhere were detested for the way they hounded and harried ships' crews, officers and men alike, while putting them through Evolutions, that is, drills for dealing with every kind of emergency such as closing up for action, misfires, ship fires, damage control, man overboard, and abandoning ship. Often First Lieutenants and even senior NCOs were made to take command as if their C.Os had become casualties.

A very large number of RNVR officers and ratings in Coastal Forces craft had been through Swinley's Circus at HMS Bee, including the notable sailor, artist and ornithologist, Peter, (later Sir Peter) Scott, a Lieutenant Commander in the RNVR. Scott's Steam Gun Boat, "Grey Goose" had accompanied the LCT's on the Dieppe raid and was for a time based in Southampton. After D-Day he visited Mastodon.

Swinley had to instil in them the dash and aggression necessary for small-boat action against German E boats and coastal convoys. But there was not much scope for dash and aggression with a cargo-carrying LCT which had to struggle to make ten knots, and whose principal armament was jokingly said to be the twelve tons of metal that made up it's bow ramp! Swinley craved action and an active service posting and he does not seem to have taken very kindly to being posted into what was

34. Captain R. Swinley (centre) and his First Lieut., Lt.Cdr C.R.Clark (right) The Wrens are believed to be the Captain's Office staff

31

essentially an administrative job in Combined Operations, which the older regular naval officers tended to regard as THE dregs.

To add to his displeasure, he inherited a ship's company comprising more Wrens than naval officers and ratings. When he assumed command it is estimated that Mastodon possessed four naval officers and sixty ratings, and three WRNS officers and well over a hundred Wrens. It grew to twenty naval officers, four warrant officers and ninety ratings, plus seven WRNS officers, about a hundred and thirty Wrens, and two nursing sisters.

Many of the Wrens and an unknown number of communication ratings were working at Lepe House which now housed not only Pugsley's Group J.1. but also elements of Group J.3. under Captain A.B.Fanshaw, RN. Some time later they had to make room for the Group J.2. staff under Captain R.J.Otway-Ruthven, RN.

The commander of the J Force Support Squadron of Gun, Flak and Rocket craft was Commander R.E.D.Ryder, V.C., RN, a veteran of both the St. Nazaire and Dieppe raids. He had won his V.C. as the naval force commander on the raid on St. Nazaire. Now aged thirty six, he had led an adventurous life. Before the war he had been on an Antarctic Expedition and at the outbreak of hostilities he had been serving in the battleship HMS Warspite. Soon afterwards he was given command of a decoy tramp steamer with hidden guns, called a Q ship, to search for enemy submarines. The ship was torpedoed on 10th June 1940 and he spent four days in the water clinging to a raft, enough to kill most men, before he was rescued. After the raids on St. Nazaire and Dieppe, and before being posted to J Force, he had briefly held command of the naval troop of the Intelligence Assault Commando, the brainchild of Ian Fleming, the creator of James Bond. This front line unit contained German linguists and former professional, including criminal, safe-crackers, to search for enemy documents and prise or blow open any safes containing them as soon as they could be captured by our advancing forces. It is tempting to speculate as to whether James Bond was partly modelled on 'Red' Ryder, who was a regular visitor to Lepe House and who was an occasional visitor to the mess at Exbury, although he and his Squadron were based at HMS Squid in Southampton and moored their craft off Hythe.

At the beginning of the year 1944, there were only ten Mark 4 LCTs moored in the Beaulieu river, six of 33rd Flotilla and four of the 35th Flotilla. By mid January the river was empty of both major landing craft and barges and it remained virtually empty until the beginning of March except for occasional visiting craft. One of the occasional visitors was LCF 4, one of the original Flak craft that had sailed to Dieppe and afterwards went to the Mediterranean. It was now attached to the 37th Flotilla, the staff of which was based at Mastodon.

In view of the growing armada of LCTs massing around the Solent at this time it is puzzling that so few craft were moored in the river. The most likely explanation is that it was a period of perpetual training for both the Army and the Navy. The Army units were learning how to reverse their vehicles on to the landing ships and craft in the

35. Commander R.E.D. Ryder VC, RN.

reverse order in which they would be disembarked, and they had to learn to drive off the vessels, through seawater and across all kinds of beach surfaces.

During exercises the previous year, there had been cause for panic when it was discovered that 64% of all vehicles could not be disembarked on the type of flat beaches that they would encounter in Normandy because when the underside of the ramps of the landing ships and craft were resting on the sand, it left an abrupt drop of over two feet off their ends, enough to damage the underside of every vehicle. All the landing ships and craft had to be hastily dispatched to shipyards all round the country to be fitted with extension flaps known as Mulock ramps. Anybody who has been on a modern car ferry will have noticed these flaps fold inboard with a crash when the main ramp is raised after loading.

The soldiers also had to get used to being at sea and learn to live aboard ships, learn emergency drills and to overcome sea-sickness. The assault troops had to learn to disembark at sea into the small assault landing craft, and they were apt to experience a very rough ride if they left their mother ships for the beach in a moderate or rough sea.

The major landing craft crews had received only a modicum of sea training and no training at all in embarking and disembarking vehicles, at their main training base at Troon, before being sent south to join one of the Assault Groups. The craft were being constructed at such a fast rate that any officer or rating with a pennyworth of experience was likely to be removed from his present craft and sent north to a shipyard to commission a new craft and act as a nucleus of 'experience' to a new crew.

The craft coming south in a continuous flow were usually manned by a crew of thirteen, two inexperienced young officers, often barely into their twenties, and eleven ratings, including two or three not very experienced NCOs and nine other ratings. They had to be 'worked up' locally and learn the basics of handling their very unwieldy vessels which had a nasty habit of turning stern into the wind because the front two thirds had no grip on the water. They had to learn how to sail and manoeuvre them in small and large formations using a special technique known as equal speed manoeuvres because the LCTs were so slow that they had insufficient speed to catch up during the normal naval formation manoeuvres. They also had to learn how and when to embark, and when and when not to disembark cargoes of men and tracked and wheeled vehicles onto the shoreline through seawater on to various types and gradients of beaches at various states of the tide, and in cross currents and cross winds. Any misjudgement on the part of the young commanding officers could be fatal to the drivers and the crews of vehicles, and to heavily laden assault troops, especially if disembarked, for instance, into unexpected deep water holes in the beach.

Anybody who has tried to beach a dinghy in a cross tide in a moderate wind will know how difficult it is to avoid being lifted up on a wave and swept sideways on to the beach. Try doing it in a 200 feet long vessel that is so shallow draughted that it has no grip on the water for most of its length! It required a lot of experience in dropping a hefty three-quarter ton stockless kedge anchor off the stern of the vessel at the right moment during the run-in to the beach.

The craft had to be 'worked up' first in their flotilla formations, then in squadron formation and ultimately, exercised in conjunction with their entire Assault Force comprising over a thousand vessels.

While the LCTs practised loading, unloading, beaching and kedging off, the Gun and Flak craft were sent to Studland Bay to learn to shoot straight and hit specific targets on the shore. Simultaneously, the Rocket craft commanding officers had to learn to navigate with pin-point accuracy with their special aircraft H2S radar navigation equipment adapted for use horizontally, so that their rockets, when fired, fell in a deadly mattress on a specified 120,000 square yards of beach.

Surprisingly, G Force, commanded by Commodore C.E.Douglas-Pennant, RN, did not come into being until

March 1944, and although its main bases were at Weymouth and Southampton, it used the Beaulieu river for mooring many of its LCT flotillas but especially for mooring its Support Squadron of Gun, Flak and Rocket craft. Consequently the officers and ratings from G Force flotillas and their senior officers, were more frequent visitors to Mastodon than their opposite numbers in J Force based at Lepe House.

Two months before D-Day Captain G.V.Dolphin, RN, who commanded Assault Group G.3., made Mastodon his headquarters and the Staff Officer (Operations) of G Force moved into the nursery of Exbury House and set up an operations room. Dolphin's command comprised mainly American Tank Landing Ships, LSTs, and Infantry Landing Craft, that is, LCI(L)s, of the Royal Canadian Navy, moored, it is believed, in the Lymington river. There must have been a continuous flow of North American officers visiting Exbury House and American and Canadian sailors plying up and down the Beaulieu river in a variety of boats.

The other assault force, S Force, was based at Portsmouth and none of its landing craft units came into the Beaulieu river.

Early in the spring of 1944 there were constant rehearsals not just for the landing craft but for all the specialised Combined Operations units that were assembling all along the south of England.

Mastodon became a transit camp, holding camp and training base for a variety of specialised units including the Royal Naval Commando, Beach Signals, Bombardment Units, spare crews for the assault craft and spare crews for the Support craft, each of which required a crew of about a dozen naval ratings to work the ship and fifty Royal Marines to man the guns. Also at Mastodon during this period were special Naval Parties, mine clearance parties, frogmen and, according to one source, a secret hydrographic survey unit. There were also frequent visits from teams of civilian and Service scientists from the Admiralty's Department of Miscellaneous Weapons Development, who experimented with all kinds of devices on the Beaulieu and Exbury estates and on the Beaulieu river.

There seems to have been a predominance of communication ratings i.e. signalman, telegraphists, coders and R/T operators, living in the barracks at

36. RN Commandos

Exbury, and they were constantly being allocated and reallocated to different units to meet various training contingencies. Some of these ratings worked at Lepe, in its signal tower, and for the planning staff, and were then posted to Cowes from where they were temporarily attached to a Beach Signals Section or a Bombardment Unit before finally sailing away in a Motor Torpedo Boat leading assault craft to a beachhead. Some were eventually drafted to Headquarters ships, like HMS Lawford.

The responsibility for organising the movement of men, vehicles and materials across the beachheads was vested in the Beachmaster organisation of the RN Commando, led by a huge, black-bearded buccaneer of a man with a stentorian voice and a ripe choice of words, Captain Colin Maud, DSO, DSC, RN. He was based at Cowes but visited his two Commando units, 'P' and 'L' Commando, each comprising 10 officers and 60 men, which arrived at Mastodon in the spring of 1944. 'L' Commando moved on but 'P' remained until it moved out for D-Day, embarking in ships at Hythe.

The Beach Signals Units, comprising thirty signalmen, telegraphists and a couple of coders, worked as part of the beaching control system, calling in the major and minor landing craft and the landing ships in an orderly and systematic manner, to discharge their cargoes. The vessels were not permitted to dump their cargoes and run to get out of the way of enemy shell fire. They had to wait their turn and be directed to the beach upon which they were scheduled to unload.

The Bombardment Units maintained communications between the bombarding warships and the Forward Observation Officers who were attached to front line units to spot the fall of shot and direct shellfire on to any enemy targets which the front line soldiers wanted destroyed.

All these 'Sailors-in-Khaki' units, so called because they wore army battledress with naval caps and badges, lived rough while working on the beachheads under constant enemy shell fire. According to one of the officers of 'P' Commando, Sub-Lieutenant Alan Dalton RNVR, (later Sir Alan Dalton), who was stationed at Exbury just prior to D-Day, they 'lived like rats in holes in the ground, with groundsheets as a roof' during the six weeks or so that they remained on the Normandy beaches, exposed to the wind, weather and exploding enemy shells.

There were three types of frogmen units in Combined Operations, manned by Royal Navy, Royal Marines and Royal Engineers swimmers. The most spectacular of these were the Combined Operations Pilotage Parties, COPPs, whose job was beach reconnaissance and surveying enemy beaches before any invasion took place, and subsequently to pilot in the approaching assault armada by marking the beaches with infra-red pilot lights and radars. Some of these units worked from the midget submarines, X 20 and X 23. Incredibly, the entire Invasion armada was spearheaded by a couple of humble old trawlers, the Dorthema and the Sapper which towed the two midget submarines across the Channel to their release positions on the 3rd or 4th of June!

The COPPs main base was on Hayling Island, but it is believed that two units of three frogmen were working for a secret hydrographic survey unit and the planners at Lepe or Exbury House. These two small units camped briefly in a field by Exbury church and are believed to have been taken across to the Normandy beaches by J or G Force MGB's prior to D-Day. On D-Day itself they went ahead of the assault troops with their radar markers.

The second type of swimmer unit was the Landing Craft Obstacle Clearance Units, called LCOCU, whose job was to clear lanes through beach obstacles, many of them mined or booby-trapped, so that the approaching landing craft could beach without being wrecked or blown up before they touched down, thereby choking the approaches with wreckage. They also had the job of blowing up or removing any landing craft which did founder or break down in the approach lanes.

There were at least two LCOCU attached to Mastodon, about forty men in all, and they camped with their lorries and equipment in the field next to Exbury church, on the opposite side of the road to the old main gate into Exbury Gardens. They and the COPP units are reported to have arrived and departed in conditions of great secrecy.

The COPP swimmers were literally the very first men of the invasion forces to land on the enemy beaches. The LCOCU reached the beaches twenty minutes after the first assault troops. There were only 120 men in all the LCOCU used in Normandy and, miraculously, only two of them were killed and ten wounded while they carried out their hazardous work on D-Day.

The third type of frogman unit was the salvage and repair units, the Landing Craft Repair and Recovery Units, LCR&RU, whose job involved surveying and repairing underwater damage to landing craft which, by the very nature of their role of beaching, were prone to damaging their propellers and stoving in their bottoms by sitting on outcrops of rock. It is fairly certain that one of these units was attached to Mastodon and was probably based at Buckler's Hard, although one source said it was located at Needs Oar Point.

There are persistent and verified reports of Motor Torpedo Boats and Motor Gun Boats being seen moored in the Beaulieu river at various stages of the war. Some of these craft were seen off Buckler's Hard earlier in the war and were probably awaiting repairs. But during the run-up to D-Day twelve boats were reported to have been lying off Gilbury pier and one source stated that they had been engaged on nefarious hydrographic and other missions.

It is known with certainty that the Captain of Coastal Forces (Channel), Captain P.V.McLaughlin, RN, visited Mastodon with his Senior Staff Officer, Commander Christopher Dreyer, RN, a very distinguished Coastal Forces officer, early in May 1944. It is also known that six MTBs or MGB's were attached to each of the assault Forces. J Force had six 'C' class MGB's, Nos. 312, 316, 317, 324, 326 and 330, all of them specially equipped with navigational aids. On Christmas Day 1943, MGB 316 commanded by Lieutenant G.D.Price, RNVR, a veteran Coastal Forces officer, had taken a three-man party of frogmen from a COPP unit to make a beach survey at Arromanche. Just before D-Day, MGB 312 was navigation leader for a small force of MGB's minelaying off the French coast at each end of the proposed landing area, to

37. C Class MGB

block off any attack on the flanks by the German Navy.

Immediately prior to D-Day the commanding officers of all six of these boats were briefed on their missions at Lepe House, and on D-Day they acted as navigational leaders for the first wave of assault landing craft.

G Force had six 'D' class MTBs of the 55th Flotilla, some of which are known to have been used to carry frogmen of COPP units across the Channel to survey enemy beaches long before D-Day.

It is highly likely that some of these craft, or HDMLs, were sent out to identify and chart enemy minefields and collect normal hydrographic data during the months preceding D-Day for J or G Force headquarters at Lepe and Exbury. Some of the MTBs may have been used to tow the COPP launching craft to the Normandy beachheads ahead of the main assault.

Towards the end of April, landing ships and craft began massing in the Solent area for several large scale assault landing exercises, and the Beaulieu river was used for mooring almost the entire Support Squadron of G Force. It must have been an impressive sight. It comprised seven Flak craft, LCFs 19, 20, 25, 26, 35, 36, and 38, six Gun craft, LCG(L)s 1, 2, 3, 13, 17, and 18, six Rocket craft, LCT(R)s 362, 434, 436, 438, 440, 459, and 460, and two flotillas of LCT(A), a total of thirty seven craft with an immense fire power. The Rocket craft collectively had the fire power of 640 cruisers and each of the Gun craft had the fire power of a small destroyer. The sixteen LCT(A) need some explanation.

As D-Day approached, General Sir Bernard Montgomery, the British Army Commander, decided that he needed more inshore fire power to silence enemy shore batteries and gun positions. It was too late to build any more Gun craft, so a considerable number of Mark 5 LCTs were converted so that the tanks or self-propelled guns that they would be carrying could fire over their gunwhales on the way in to the beaches. After unloading the tanks or guns they could revert to cargo carrying.

The Mark 5 LCT was an American invention. It had a loaded displacement of just over 300 tons and was 80 feet shorter than the British LCTs but just as beamy. It had been designed to be carried on the backs of American landing ships as cargo and slipped over the side once it reached a far-away landing area. It was meant for ship to

38. Landing Craft Gun (Large) off Hurst Castle

shore work and had only primitive accommodation for its crew. One hundred and sixty of them had been shipped to this country for use by the Royal Navy. Each one arrived in three sections and had to be put together on arrival; many of them were assembled in Southampton

Their appearance with the G Force Support Squadron was the first time that these craft, and the Rocket craft, were seen in the Beaulieu river but after D-Day both types became a familiar sight on the moorings. The sixteen Mark 5 Assault craft belonged to the 108th and

39. King George VI taking the salute of Assault Landing Craft at Cowes Castle shortly before D-Day

docks. They had a speed of only five knots but they could carry four heavy army tanks, one more than the old Mark 2 LCTs that had been used at Dieppe.

Although they had been intended only for ship to shore work, both the Royal Navy and the American Navy used them for ocean passages, usually by towing them behind landing ships before releasing them for ship to shore work in the assault areas. But they were not very seaworthy when converted to LCT(A)s. The conversion involved raising their tank decks so that the tanks or artillary they were carrying could fire over their fo'c's'les and gunwhales. But once three ancient Centaur tanks or self-propelled guns were put aboard with their extra ammunition, the craft were overloaded and became unstable and liable to founder. On D-Day they crossed the Channel under their own steam and ten of them foundered in the bad weather.

109th LCT Flotillas.

The last major rehearsal for D-Day was called Exercise Fabius and it took place from the 2nd to the 6th May. All the army units were previously embarked from ports and jetties all along the coast and the vehicles were embarked from hards all over the area, including Q Hard at Lepe. Each Force made for a different part of the south coast to practise their landings. G Force went to Hayling Island, J Force to Bracklesham Bay, just outside Chichester harbour, and S Force went to Littlehampton.

The Americans had held their final rehearsal on 26th April at Slapton Sands and during the night preceding the exercise a force of German E boats got in among the convoy of landing ships and torpedoed several of them causing the loss of life of over six hundred American servicemen. The E boats escaped unscathed, unaware that they had witnessed a rehearsal for the invasion, believing that they had just attacked a coastal convoy of freighters.

Fabius has been proclaimed a success by some writers and described as a shambles by others. It was followed by several smaller scale exercises up to the beginning of June.

The G Force Support Squadron returned to the Beaulieu river after Fabius and was joined by sixty craft of B Squadron of LCVP assault craft and by twelve rather antiquated assault craft known as LCPR of 476 Ancillary Flotilla. All the minor craft were moored between Buckler's Hard and Gilbury Hard, and the personnel for them, over 250 officers and men, plus their staffs and maintenance personnel, were accommodated at Mastodon, some, probably, in the Master Builder's House hotel. It is thought that it was one of these men who carved the inscription into an oak beam over one of the hotel's fireplaces.

A week before D-Day there were about 1,500 Naval personnel and Royal Marines and upwards of 500 Canadian Commandos living under canvas on the lawns and in the woods of the Exbury estate, being fed from three field kitchens. In addition, there were 70 officers and men of 'P' RN Commando plus about 90 ratings of the base staff and miscellaneous units living in the barracks, over 2,300 personnel in all.

Similarly on the Beaulieu side of the river the woods were full of encamped soldiers from the 50th Division and the 3rd Canadian Division.

On 24th May, or thereabouts, HMS Mastodon received a visit from His Majesty King George VIth. Captain Swinley, for reasons known only to himself, ordered all the Wrens to make themselves scarce and they were hidden in the House and the barracks when the King arrived to inspect a Royal Marines guard of honour, and the troops. Afterwards many of those present expressed amazement at discovering that the King appeared to be wearing make-up! He spent some time strolling through the gardens, which he knew well, before walking down to Gilbury pier to board his royal barge and sailing down the river to visit many of the ships moored in the Solent and other encampments in the area.

His visit was taken as a sign that D-Day was imminent.

40. King George VI, Commodore C. E. Douglass-Pennant and Admiral Ramsey inspecting sailors aboard a ship in the Solent

CHAPTER 5
NEVIL SHUTE AND THE MYSTERY BOMBER

A former Wren stated that Nevil Shute, or, to give him his correct name and title, Lieutenant Commander Nevil Shute Norway, RNVR, was working at Exbury with a team of Service and civilian scientist in February 1944. He was already a popular novelist and some of his books had been made into Hollywood films. The Wren trot boat crews used to take him and the scientists down the river to the mud flats near Exbury Point to carry out experiments with rockets and rocket launchers, and later down to the opposite side of the river, to Needs Oar Point. The men used to borrow gum boots from the Wrens to walk about in the mud.

It is also rumoured that he used to take his young Wren girlfriend at Mastodon out to tea at a teashop that used to be situated in one of the cottages close to Hatchet Pond. Her surname was said to be Prentice, the name he gave to his heroine in his novel "Requiem for a Wren".

There can be no doubt, after reading "Requiem", about a third of which is about HMS Mastodon during the period of the run-up to the invasion, that he must have spent some time at Exbury and upon the Beaulieu river. The novel is littered with accurate domestic and naval details that could only have been known to somebody who had spent much time there. For instance, he knew that the Rothschild's gardeners were still employed there and was aware of their complaints about ratings breaking into the glass houses and stealing rare blooms to give to their Wren girl friends. He is also scrupulously accurate in identifying various Marks of tank landing craft that moored in the river at this time and even the identification numbers he mentions in the book were real and correct for particular Marks of craft.

He knew of the mysterious German bomber that crashed at Lower Exbury a few weeks before D-Day and accurately identified it as a Junkers 188, as distinct from the more commonplace Junkers 88, and gave an accurate description of the site of the crash and of the wreckage. He is even correct about the month in which it was shot down, but is inaccurate about the time of day of the crash. Above all, he knew of the mystery of its crew of seven in an aircraft built for a crew of four. Unless he had been present, he could not have known that many of the dead airmen had Slavic, not Germanic surnames. It gave him plenty of scope for speculating in his novel about the nature of their mission. This single incident in the spring of 1944 provides the very core of the plot of "Requiem for a Wren", first published in 1955.

However, he is surprisingly vague about Support craft and does not distinguish between the various types. He is

41. Lt-Cdr. Nevil Shute Norway, RNVR in his office at the Admiralty

also remarkably restrained and coy with his description of Captain Swinley who is alleged to have given his officers a hard time, asserting his authority in countless demeaning ways. Shute is known to have had a particular aversion to authoritarian naval officers, especially senior naval officers.

So, what was Shute doing at Exbury, and when did he first arrive there?

His autobiography, "Slide Rule", written in 1953, does not relate his career beyond the year 1938 and gives no hints about what he had been doing during the war, except to mention casually in the foreword that he was commissioned as a Lieutenant in the RNVR in 1940 and was assigned to duties at the Admiralty in London.

The Navy List reveals that he was working in the Department of Miscellaneous Weapons Development, DMWD. It was staffed by a motley collection of Service and civilian scientists, colloquially known as the Wheezers and Dodgers, who experimented with an enormous variety of devices, by no means all of them related to weaponry.

In 1956 a description of some of the work of this Department was published by Gerald Pawle in his book "The Secret War", but because of the way the material is structured it is impossible to ascertain the dates on which trials took place of particular devices. Although this book has a foreword by Nevil Shute, he does not refer to his own part in the activities of DMWD, and Pawle gives few clues in the text.

However, from a variety of other sources it is clear that Shute was a senior and influential member of the Department and was aware of all its projects. He, personally, managed many of them and did some of the detailed design work on some projects, such as the projectors on the LCT(R) and both the projectiles and the projectors on a smaller version called the LCA (Hedgerow).

It has not been possible from available sources to determine exactly when he first appeared at Exbury, or to identify which projects first brought him there, or to discover why Exbury and the Beaulieu river were selected for the trials of some devices in preference to the twelve or so proving grounds round the Welsh, Devon, Dorset and Hampshire coasts known to have been used by DMWD during various stages of the war.

In 1976, Julian Smith, an American academic from San Diego State University, published a literary review and appreciation of the work of Nevil Shute, and in passing gives a number of clues about Shute's wartime activities as well as providing revealing information about the man himself and how he composed his novels. It also reveals that Shute's private papers and his wartime diary are lodged in the National Library of Australia.

Shute's autobiography reveals that soon after the first world war he took a very modest third class honours degree in Engineering at Oxford University and in 1923 took his first job as a stress engineer with the De Havilland Aircraft Company. He was already writing novels in his spare time and published his first in 1926. From the time he graduated until 1938 he continued working in the aircraft industry on aircraft and airships, eventually becoming co-founder of the firm Airspeed Limited. Simultaneously he wrote and published several novels, one of which, "Lonely Road", was made into a Hollywood film.

From 1938 until he joined the RNVR he worked almost full time as a novelist, occasionally leaving his writing to do casual experimental work on rockets and gliding torpedoes with Sir Dennistoun Burney. As a keen yachtsman he volunteered for the Navy, at the age of 41, hoping for a sea-going appointment. He was most indignant when, after being commissioned at HMS King Alfred, the RNVR officers training school at Hove, he was posted to the Admiralty to continue his work on the selfsame weapons that he had been experimenting with before joining up.

He was soon involved with engineering problems associated with the manufacture in Britain of the newly acquired Swiss invention, the 20mm Oerlikon light anti-aircraft gun. It was to become the standard defensive weapon on all tank landing craft. His interest in this gun provided the inspiration for making his heroine in "Requiem for a Wren" an armourer. In fact there were no Wren armourers at Mastodon.

DMWD moved to several different offices in central London until it came to rest in the old Automobile Association HQ in Leicester Square. Initially, the war in the Atlantic dominated the attention of the Department because of the pressing need for anti-aircraft and anti-submarine weapons.

Shute experimented at Dartmouth with flame throwers for the defence of ships against both aircraft and surface vessels, but they proved to be very dangerous for the operators, and the idea was dropped. However, it provided Shute with material for his novel "Most Secret", which the Admiralty refused to allow him to publish during the war.

Early in the war he headed a team of scientists experimenting with rockets. Rocketry solutions were found for the defence of ships against both aircraft and submarines. The anti-aircraft weapon was called the Potato Thrower and the anti-submarine device was nicknamed the Hedgehog; it was a multi-barrelled mortar that hurled heavy rocket-bombs into the sea several hundred yards ahead of the vessel. Shute also directed research into de-salination plants for life boats.

From the earliest days of Combined Operations he worked on various gadgets 'to assist the landings that were being planned for France', by which he meant devices to overcome enemy beach and cliff defences and shore batteries. Practically all of these were rockets or rocket-propelled devices and systems for their delivery, including unmanned drone aircraft. One of his personal inventions is said to be the rocket-propelled grappling iron used by cliff-climbing commandos. It was first tested on the cliffs at Freshwater Bay on the Isle of Wight, where, to this day, the Services train people to climb the chalk cliffs.

Prior to August 1942 much of the experimental work of his department took place at Portsmouth, but in August it was moved to the Combined Operations Experimental Establishment at Appledore. Later Shute moved about the south coast to watch the trials of many rocket-propelled weapons, few of which were adopted by the Services. One spectacular failure was a huge invention called the Catherine Wheel, a monstrous device driven by rockets that was meant to roll off the ramp of an LCT and up a beach before exploding.

Judging by what Shute wrote in "Requiem for a Wren", he made his first appearance at Exbury in the late autumn of 1943. He had by this time been promoted to the rank of Lieutenant Commander. His description of the living conditions at Exbury prior to this date, and of the craft lying in the river are, uncharacteristically, inaccurate, indicating that he had learned of them at second hand, or had made an informed guess. But his description of events from the winter of 1943 until the invasion in 1944, could only have been written by someone who paid regular visits to Mastodon and lived there for protracted periods.

Lord Montagu and several local people recall seeing a 'model' aircraft flying off Needs Oar Point in the autumn of 1943. This was in fact part of the trials of one of Shute's pet projects, a rocket-propelled pilotless aircraft called the Swallow which weighed nearly seven hundredweight.

Soon after the Dieppe raid the Services asked DMWD if it was possible to make a pilotless aircraft that could fly along a heavily defended enemy beach at an altitude of 200 feet laying a curtain of smoke to conceal an approaching assault landing. It was considered suicidal to do this with an ordinary manned aircraft.

Nevil Shute had already spent much time inventing and developing gliders and scale model aircraft for use as targets for practising anti-aircraft gun crews. He went down to Farnborough to the Royal Aircraft Establishment and in conjunction with them developed the Swallow from a target plane.

It was described by other engineers and scientists as a "brilliantly ingenious" invention, propelled by fifteen slow-burning rockets and controlled by a clockwork mechanism in the tailplane, rather like the mechanism of a fairly modern washing machine which mechanically controls many sequential operations. But the Swallow had to be catapulted into the air at 100 mph from a trolley after a run of only 40 feet; why this distance had to be so short is unknown.

The trolley proved to be a very difficult proposition. A similar device had already been produced by DMWD for an idea being developed by Barnes Wallis, the inventor of the earthquake bomb and the spinning bomb used by the RAF Dambusters to destroy the German dams.

Trials of the Swallow's launcher began at Worthy Down near Winchester, probably early in 1943 and later moved to Brean Down on the coast near DMWD's proving ground at Weston-Super-Mare. In the autumn the trials moved to the Beaulieu river, for unknown reasons.

The earlier trials revealed that it needed twenty rockets to accelerate the trolley, which weighed nearly half a ton, to 100 mph in a distance of 40 feet, and it struck its buffers with a force of 80 tons. One can only imagine the difficulties of inventing hydraulic buffers to withstand such a force.

For the trials in the Beaulieu river, the necessary 40 feet of track and the buffers were fitted to the deck of an obsolete landing craft, probably an old Mark 2 LCT, which must also have been fitted with a small crane capable of lifting about a ton. The LCT was moored below Gins farm, in the last long reach of the river so that when the aircraft crashed it could be recovered from the marshes at Needs Oar Point.

The first trials in the river were to determine the exact speed of the trolley when it hit the buffers. The weight of the trolley when it was loaded with Swallow was nearly three quarters of a ton, the weight of a small saloon car. To avoid repeatedly launching the precious aircraft into the marshes and risk damaging it unnecessarily, a series of dummy runs were made using concrete blocks of the same weight, 750 lbs. Any outsider witnessing these trials must have wondered what purpose was being served by pitching massive concrete blocks into the Beaulieu river at 100 mph, off a trolley belching flames and smoke from its 20 rockets.

Great difficulties were experienced in making reliable measurements with the instruments that had been placed aboard the LCT to measure the speed of the trolley on impact with the buffers. Day after day the trials continued and tons of concrete blocks were pitched into the river before it was discovered that the instruments were faulty!

Even when the faults were corrected and the launching speed was ascertained, trials with the pilotless aircraft produced faults in the control mechanism which caused the plane to wobble in flight and plunge into the marshes. After many trials it was discovered that the immense acceleration of the catapult trolley was upsetting the aircraft's delicate mechanical guidance mechanism. Once this was corrected the Swallow flew, climbed and banked beautifully.

Unfortunately, by this time, probably February or March 1944, it was too near to D-Day to get the device into production. The Swallow was never used during the war, but afterwards the data produced by the Beaulieu river trials was used for the development of early guided weapons, the forerunners of Cruise Missiles.

From Shute's own writings he was evidently at Mastodon in March 1944 and witnessed the futile attempt by a team from Mastodon to rescue a soldier drowning in an army tank that had dropped off the ramp of an LCT into a hole in the beach at Newtown in the Isle of Wight. Early in April he witnessed the shooting down of a German aircraft at Exbury. These two incidents are faithfully recorded in "Requiem".

Although in the novel the German plane was shot down by a Wren using a 20mm Oerlikon gun on an LCT, the reality is very different. Through the good offices of the Air Historical Branch it has been possible to obtain the real story of the mystery bomber that crashed in the grounds of Exbury House, at Lower Exbury at 7.45 a.m. on 18th April 1944.

The aircraft was first picked up by our radar when it was halfway between Le Havre and St. Catherine's Point on the Isle of Wight. Flying north at 4,000 feet, it crossed the Hampshire coast near the estuary of the Beaulieu river and flew a complete circuit over the Isle of Wight.

The anti-aircraft guns on the Island, and the guns of many thousands of ships and craft lying in the Solent fired at it whenever it came into their range and it started firing clusters of red Verey lights.

Two RAF Typhoon fighters of 266 Squadron, piloted by Flight Lieutenant A.V.Saunders and Flight Sergeant D.H.Dodd, appeared upon the scene and engaged the German bomber, which fired back at them. They chased it twice over Exbury before it caught fire and started coming down. As it passed very low over the Exbury estate, the men of the RN Commando rushed out of the barracks at Mastodon firing their Bren guns at it. The bomber had been riddled by the fighters and the preceding anti-aircraft gunfire before it finally crashed.

A Petty Officer of the RN Commando is credited with being the first on the scene of the crash and began pulling the airmen from the blazing wreckage. Some reports say that one of the airmen was still alive, others say that two were still alive but very badly wounded. They were taken to the sick bay at Mastodon where they died.

The rescuers were very surprised to find seven men in an aircraft built for a crew of four. To add to the mystery, all the dead airmen were Unteroffiziers i.e. Luftwaffe Corporals, all very young, between 20 and 23 years of age. The surnames of four of them were Slavic and the other three were Germanic. They were all buried in the churchyard of All Saints church at Fawley, with full military honours, and lay there until 1963 when the bodies were removed to the Central German War Cemetary at Cannock Chase in Staffordshire.

The 'kill' is officially credited to the anti-aircraft gunners and the two Typhoons.

The official interpretation of their flight will remain a secret for 75 years because of a tradition which respects the feelings of relatives of war dead in cases where the integrity of the dead men is supect. In this instance it is suspect because it was rumoured at the time that they

42. A JU 188 German Bomber, similar to the one shot down at Exbury

were trying to surrender, which is the explanation given by Nevil Shute in "Requiem". It would therefore be unkind to name the seven dead men.

However, the following information has been released by the Air Historical Branch and was obtained, presumably after the war, from the records of the Luftwaffe.

Four of the dead men were the crew of the aircraft, one was from the crew of another aircraft and two were technical ground staff. It was strictly forbidden by the Luftwaffe to carry more than five people in a JU 188. It is also thought unlikely that seven corporals could have conspired to desert without being discovered by the ubiquitous German security networks.

The five aircrew men had boarded the plane that morning with the intention of transferring from one air base to another. The two technicians are thought to have hitched a lift, against all official orders.

There was a very thick ground mist at the time of the flight and it is very probable that the crew completely lost their bearings. A senior RAF officer has confirmed that it was not unusual for both German and British aircrew to lose their bearings.

It was the firing of the red Verey lights when the aircraft was attacked with gunfire that gave rise to the rumour that the seven men were trying to desert. A kinder interpretation would be that when they realised their predicament through a navigational error they tried to indicate that they meant no harm. As there was no Air Force equivalent to waving a white flag for a truce, they fired the Verey lights.

It was tragic that they appeared over the Solent at a time when it was packed with invasion ships and craft and everything possible was being done to conceal our intentions. It is surprising that it was not shot down long before it was anywhere near the Solent area which, at this time, seven weeks before D-Day, must have been one of the most heavily defended parts of the country.

Nevil Shute, who used the incident as the core of the plot of "Requiem", wrote at least four other novels during his war service. When the Admiralty refused permission for the publication of "Most Secret", Shute was furious and wrote scathing letters to the most senior Naval officers at the Admiralty. They retaliated by giving him so much work to do that he had no time for any writing during 1943.

In the late spring of 1944, at about the time of the trials with the Swallow pilotless aircraft, he was appointed as a war correspondent to the Ministry of Information and it was in this role that he must have spent the run-up to D-Day at Mastodon. It explains how he found the time to gain an intimate knowledge of events at Exbury and on the Beaulieu river during this period. But he was not in the locality at the beginning of June.

His diary recorded that on 1st June he was called away from flight trials with a new weapon and travelled to Southampton by train a couple of days later. On 3rd June he went shopping for a book in Southampton before embarking as a war correspondent in a vessel that sailed with the invasion armada on the aborted start on 5th June.

He stayed in Normandy for about a week before returning to London to continue his work at the Admiralty. In the winter of 1944 he flew to Burma as a war correspondent.

Shute's novels are all very readable and his plots usually highlighted social injustice or bureaucratic disdain of technical expertise, as in "No Highway", which in truth foretold aircraft crashes through airframe fatigue, which was officially dismissed as speculative nonsense at the time. But literary critics ignored his work despite its huge popularity, possibly because it was too close to reportage in plot and style, and lacked real imagination and creativity.

However it was conceded that his novels gave remarkably reliable portraits of the life and times about which he wrote. Indeed, his attention to accuracy of detail was usually punctilious.

Today's casual readers of his novels are unlikely to be aware of this unless they lived during the times and in the places he portrayed. They have no means of knowing whether they are reading pure fiction or a story firmly anchored in fact, what in today's terms is called 'faction'.

There is no doubt that "Requiem" is faction. In the story, the Wren, Janet Prentice, is an armourer servicing the Oerlikon guns of the tank landing craft lying in the Beaulieu river. She is also a sure shot and when a Junkers 188 bomber strays over the Solent she fires a gun of the craft on which she happens to be working and shoots it down. Subsequently she is taken to inspect the wreckage and discovers that she has killed seven Poles and Czechs trying to escape from Germany to fight on our side. This tragedy, heaped upon other personal losses of family and friends, preys upon her mind and years later, after the war, she commits suicide while working in Australia.

It is far from being one of Shute's best novels. It is a re-working of plots and characters that he had used in several previous stories that he had written as far back as 1946, and it originally had the title of "Blind Understanding". He was puzzled by its lack of success and once commented to a friend that it was extraordinary that no one seemed to notice that "Requiem" was the same story as "A Town Like Alice", the former with a tragic ending and the latter a happy one. He does not seem to have realised that whereas "Requiem's" theme was one of despair, "Alice" portrayed a triumph of the human spirit.

"A Town Like Alice" is about women prisoners of war in the hands of the Japanese in the second world war and it is one of his best and most successful novels. Unlike "Requiem" which hinges on a single brief incident and a patchwork of background events, "Alice" is based upon a wonderful true story of a woman's survival in the face of great adversity. It is in fact based upon the real life story of a 21 year old Dutch woman Mrs. Geysel, who, with her six months old baby was made prisoner by the Japanese in the Dutch East Indies. With 80 other women and hoards of children they were forced to walk 1,200 miles through the jungles of Sumatra. At the end of it nearly all the other women and children had died, but Mrs Geysel and her baby survived and came out of their ordeal fit and well, still retaining her sense of humour, and was reunited with her husband.

"Alice" was written in 1949, and has since been filmed and made into a very popular television series staring Helen Morse, an Australian actress. Shute did not begin writing "Requiem" until 1953 and it took him three years to complete it. For all its faults it does give an excellent description of life at HMS Mastodon during the months before and after D-Day, and accurately recaptures the language, spirit and conditions of those times.

Nevil Shute died on 12th January 1960, in Australia, where he emigrated soon after the war. He was 61 years of age.

CHAPTER 6
NEPTUNE'S TRIDENT

Anybody who has seen the Operations Orders for Operation Neptune, the Navy's part in the invasion of Normandy, will marvel at their bulk and complexity. The main Orders, printed on foolscap paper, now discolouring with age, are two inches thick and cover every aspect of the operation starting with clearing passages through offshore German minefields to the landing of the First and Second Allied Armies. They include the subsequent seaward protection of the beachheads and their western and eastern flanks from German counter-attacks by aircraft, submarines, surface ships and E boats, mines and other nasty devices, and cover every conceivable contingency including poison gas attacks. They also include the scale and pace of the build-up once the beachheads had been secured.

In addition to the main Operation Orders, each Force commander issued his own very detailed Orders. The G Force Orders are almost as bulky as the main Orders; the J Force Orders are half the bulk but still substantial. Each Force Orders tell every vessel in the armada, down to the smallest assault craft and barges, when and where to load, where to moor to await sailing orders, when to sail, where to rendezvous for passage across the Channel, which passage to use, which beach to lay off or land upon in Normandy and at what time to start bombarding or make their landings. They tell every vessel, especially the smaller ones, where to go to draw fuel, ammunition and rations once they reach the invasion area. They even instruct the crews of the kitchen barges not to issue rum rations to the crews of craft pulling alongside for hot food, and not to allow the crews of the visiting craft to

43. Neptune operation orders (the main Orders are on the right)

remain aboard while eating their meals, thereby preventing other craft from coming alongside.

Considering that over 7,000 vessels were under way, including the often forgotten 900 merchant vessels, and hundreds, if not thousands of bits of the Mulberry harbours were being towed by over a hundred tugs and numerous ships and landing craft, the Orders are a miracle of detailed planning and especially of timing to allow for the huge range of speed, or lack of it, of everything afloat. Every ship, craft and thing had to arrive off Normandy at the right state of the tide, at the right times and in the right sequence.

The logistics of getting the huge armada of vessels out of the Solent without collision or getting muddled with the wrong convoy and Force were miraculous. In the event, G Force left by the west Solent, J Force went out through Spithead, and S Force left from Portsmouth and ports further east.

There were three prongs to Neptune's Trident, that is, roughly three classes of vessels involved in the assault. First, there were the fighting ships, the warships, from battleships down to torpedo boats, minesweepers and the landing craft Support Squadrons of Gun, Flak and Rocket craft. Their job was to bombard the shore installations and defend the assault from sea and air counter-attack. Second, there were the assault landing ships and craft, carrying the assault troops and assault vehicles, including swimming tanks and special vehicles dubbed Hobart's Funnies to deal with beach minefields. After the assault these vessels became the cross-Channel Shuttle Service to ferry the build-up forces. The third prong was the Ferry Craft Units, comprising small vessels such as assault boats, LCVPs, LCMs, barges, DUKW's (amphibious lorries) and massive pontoons with equally massive outboard motors called Rhinos. These followed close behind the assault forces for ship to shore ferrying of men and materials. The interesting thing about these little vessels is that a very large number of them crossed the Channel under their own steam and in bad weather on D-Day and the days that followed.

All three prongs of the Trident were represented by the various types of craft that lay in the Beaulieu river in the run-up to D-Day and many vital ancillary units were

44. Massed tank landing craft at Southampton docks prior to D-Day

waiting at Mastodon for the signal to commence Operation Neptune.

The final details for the invasion were settled early in May 1944 and during the next few weeks there was hectic activity afloat and ashore. Millions of British, Canadian and American troops, and the troops of many other Allied nationalities were on the move southwards to their pre-embarkation positions all along the south of England, unaware that the date for the invasion had been fixed for the 5th June.

During the first two weeks in May, Admiral Sir Bertram Ramsey left his headquarters at Southwick House to stay at Exbury House for five days, during which he held conferences for a large number of senior Naval officers to discuss many major aspects of the operation. According to one source, there was much discussion about the timing of the landings and the earliest time that the Germans would be able to see the silhouettes of the approaching armada. There had to be enough daylight for the LCOCU swimmers to do their hazardous work along the enemy shoreline which was thick with mined and booby trapped obstacles and minefields, and also light enough for the sea and air bombardments to be accurate.

Ramsey also included in the conference a meeting of the commanding officers and the gunnery officers of the bombarding warships to discuss such matters as the fusing of different types of shells to make them effective against the enemy concrete fortifications. This meeting was attended by the captains of battleships and cruisers and smaller vessels down to the Squadron Commanders of the Gun, Flak and Rocket craft.

The officers attending the conference travelled to Exbury by road or were collected from ships moored all over the Solent and brought up the Beaulieu river to Gilbury pier and thence to Exbury House. It must have been a spectacular parade of gold braid and notable Naval personalities. It included the G and J Force Commanders, Commodores C.E.Douglas-Pennant and G.N.Oliver, brought over from Cowes, and their Assault Group Captains, including A.F.Pugsley, (who was J.1.), and G.V.M.Dolphin, (who was G.3.).

Before Admiral Ramsey left Mastodon, all the Wrens, ratings and marines waiting there for D-Day, over 2,000 of them, were gathered into the daffodil field, a hillock on the

45. Commadore G. N. Oliver RN, J Force Commander

Exbury estate overlooking the Beaulieu river, to hear an open air address from Ramsey about the massive enterprise upon which they were about to embark.

By early May, the three J Force Assault Group Captains were working from Lepe House and at least two of the G Force Assault Group Captains, including G.V.M.Dolphin, and probably Captain F.A.Ballance RN had installed themselves in Exbury House with their staffs of Naval and WRNS officers and their large staffs of Wrens. One of the major embarkation areas for troops and vehicles being carried by G Force craft was Stanswood Bay (between Lepe and Calshot) where, on the foreshore there was a satellite base administered by Mastodon. Another G Force loading area was at Calshot where assault troops were embarked in LCI(L)'s brought round from the Lymington river.

The officers' mess at Mastodon was so crowded that many of the junior male officers on the base staff were moved out of the House and the huts into tents to make room for their seniors. Similarly, the G Force WRNS officers and many of their Wrens were accommodated in billets in Exbury and Beaulieu villages. The Montagu Arms hotel was unable to house the influx.

All those who lived through this period speak of the frantic activites taking place at Mastodon and of working very long hours, seventeen or more hours each day. One of the WRNS officers of J.2. Group wrote, "Often I walked to my cottage across the tented lawns after midnight, the troops having long since turned in. Often at dinner we had our coffee first, to save time," before returning to work into the night.

The embarkation of men and vehicles into the ships began two weeks before D-Day. By the end of May the Canadian Commandos, the RN Commandos, the frogmen, the marines and numerous signal units had moved out of the tents at Mastodon into what many of them described as 'concentration camps' on Southampton Common and elsewhere, where they were sealed off for security reasons to await embarkation at the docks.

At Exbury a troop of 40 Royal Marines arrived to seal off Mastodon and prevent the base staff and the remaining units from having any contact with the local civilian population.

The Gun, and Flak craft of the G Force Support Squadron moved out of the Beaulieu river to Southampton and Portsmouth to load huge quantities of ammunition and afterwards anchored in Southampton water to await the signal to sail. Four Rocket craft, Nos, 362, 440, 459, and 460, of the 332nd Support Flotilla returned to the Beaulieu river after taking on over 2,000 rockets apiece from ammunition trains at Southampton docks. The two Mark 5 LCT(A) flotillas, the 108th and 109th, left to embark their Centaur tanks and self propelled guns, and ammunition, probably at Q Hard at Lepe, and the 108th and half of the 109th returned to their Beaulieu river moorings after loading.

Upriver from Gilbury pier lay the 60 craft of the Royal Marines 'B' Squadron of LCVPs, now described as a Follow-up Squadron and about twelve of the ancient LCPR assault boats, called the 476 Ancillary Flotilla.

Mastodon, which a few days previously had been seething with people, was plunged into comparative

46. A rocket craft being loaded with ammunition at Southampton docks

inactivity. The hectic planning, the kitting out of sailors and marines with protective clothing, issuing them with ration packs and storing all the major landing craft with food and other supplies, suddenly ceased. The Wrens of the planning staffs had nothing more to do; the male members of the planning staffs had all gone, embarked in HMS Bulolo, HMS Lawford and many other Headquarters ships and craft. The male and female members of the flotilla staffs could do nothing but wait, their tasks complete until their craft returned, if they returned, from Normandy.

One of the very last ratings left in the tented camp on the lawns of Exbury House stated that all that remained of the personnel was a small detatchment of marines who were taking down the tents. But the barracks were evidently full of base staff, swollen by the extra staff that had been drafted in to help cope with the final preparations. The solitary rating and a supernumary petty officer had nowhere to sleep once the tents had been struck and spent three nights in a garden shed before themselves embarking for Normandy as part of No. 3 Bombardment Unit.

Once the troops, sailors and marines had been moved into sealed camps, the final briefing began of the Squadron, Flotilla and commanding officers of thousands of ships and craft. The briefing took place in Southampton's Guildhall and lasted five days.

47. A rocket craft firing

On Sunday 4th June, Wren Jean Watson in Mastodon's signals office in the basement of Exbury House, was the first person on the base to receive the signal to sail.

That evening Captain Roland Swinley, RN, the Commanding Officer of HMS Mastodon, stood at a point overlooking the lower reaches of the Beaulieu river to watch the major landing craft of the Support Squadron, the Rocket craft and the LCT(A)s, slip their moorings and sail out of the river into the Solent. At 9 p.m. he stood at the end of Gilbury pier to take the salute as the sixty craft of 'B' Squadron of LCVPs left their moorings and sailed past the pier and down the river, heading for Normandy under their own steam. Each of the 36 feet long open craft was manned by three Royal Marines, some carrying in addition, their Flotilla officers.

Captain Swinley permitted members of the ship's company of Mastodon, including the Wrens, to go down

51

to the river to watch the major and minor craft depart. Many of the Wrens were weeping as they watched their boyfriends and the craft leave, and they all had very mixed feelings, relieved that all the preparations and the waiting were over, anxious for the safety of the crews, many dreading that the whole enterprise might turn into a bloody fiasco.

As is well known, the weather was so bad that the invasion was postponed for 24 hours. 'B' Squadron of LCVPs received the signal postponing their departure just one hour after sailing down the Beaulieu river and were ordered to anchor off Hayling Island. The crews, soaked with spray from the rough seas whipped up by the high winds, spent a very wet and uncomfortable night and the daylight hours of the following day at their anchorage before finally receiving the signal to proceed.

When the decision to delay was made because of bad weather, many warships, especially the minesweepers, had already sailed. In fact the minesweepers had already begun sweeping channels through the German minefields when the signal reached them ordering them to turn back. Mercifully, because the radio and radar countermeasures had already started, the Germans remained ignorant of what was about to happen.

In the Solent, the awaiting armada spent a very anxious and uncomfortable time bouncing about at their anchorages, dragging their anchors in the high winds.

48. Mark 5 LCT

Because of the delay the men had devoured much of the rations with which they had been supplied for the voyage. In order that they should arrive at the beachheads with adequate food, they were re-issued with ration packs and were ordered to dispose of those already broken into. Apparently much of the uneaten rations were dumped over the side into the Solent and for weeks afterwards the local population were harvesting the unexpected bounty washed on to accessible beaches.

The armada sailed on the evening of 5th June and arrived off Normandy at first light on June 6th.

Once they set sail, all the ships and craft, thousands of them, had orders not to stop for anything or anybody. Many of the craft foundered. Ten overloaded Mark 5 LCT(A)s turned over and sank, as did many barges and smaller vessels. Of the 45 small rocket craft called LCA(Hedgerow), that were being towed, only 12 reached the beachheads and some of these blew their bottoms out when they fired their two dozen heavy mortar bombs to clear the beaches of mines. Their enormous rocket-bombs had been one of Nevil Shute's brainchilds.

before sailing for France.

At 10 p.m. on June 6th, D-Day, a Rocket craft from J Force, probably LCT(R) 405, returned to the Beaulieu river, watched by Wrens and ratings from Mastodon as she sailed to her moorings blackened by burned rocket

49. The Phoenix's in position in the Mulberry Harbour in Normandy.

With so many small craft foundering, many of their crews drowned before they could be rescued by the American Coast Guard Cutters, ten of which had been assigned to each Force for rescue purposes.

After the main assault on the Normandy beaches, the empty landing ships and craft returned to load with more troops and vehicles, thus beginning the weary routine of the Shuttle Service, sailing from France at night and returning, loaded, by day to minimise the risks to loaded convoys of night attacks by German E boats.

Before the assaulting ships and craft returned, follow-up vessels and craft were leaving in convoys. After the main Assault Forces had sailed, the estuary of the Beaulieu river was used as an assembly area for six massive 'Phoenix' caissons. At 2 a.m. on the morning of June 6th, 16 barges left the river for France; 10 more left at 4 a.m. On D plus 8, sixty two barges assembled in the river

propellant, "her crew exhausted but otherwise unharmed." Once the assault phase was over the Rocket craft had no more to do and most returned to their home bases once the beachheads had been established. It is not known for certain why 405 returned so soon, unless it was due to some sort of electrical or mechanical failure. But it is known, with certainty, that when she fired her rockets, the vibration of the blast smashed all her crockery!

On the other side of the Channel, the Germans did not sit in their bunkers wringing their hands. They struck back with every weapon at their disposal, from the land, in the air, on the sea and under it.

Although greatly outnumbered, the Luftwaffe attacked the assault forces and one of the first casualties was Captain Pugsley's Headquarters ship, HMS Lawford. She was hit by a bomb on the night of 7th June, breaking her back before she sank and left her crew struggling in the sea in the dark. Pugsley was rescued by a minesweeper. His job as Captain of J.1. Assault Group had ceased once the beaches were secure. He then became deputy to Rear Admiral Sir Phillip Vian and also became Captain (Patrols). The latter job entailed organising Coastal Forces craft and minesweepers into a defensive line for the inshore protection of the eastern flank of the invasion beaches. He was inspecting the line when HMS Lawford was bombed. After he was rescued he suffered from hypothermia but nevertheless in borrowed clothes he spent a couple of days working ashore before he found the opportunity to return to Mastodon to collect his own clothes which he had left with Captain Swinley. He did not return to Normandy until later that month.

Meanwhile the eastern flank was ferociously attacked every day by German shore batteries and every night by E boats using torpedoes and mines, and by minelaying aircraft. Pugsley later stated that a 'fantastic' number of mines had been laid off the beachheads, more than the Germans had laid in their regular minefield. In his autobiography he reveals that he, and all those who worked afloat off the beaches, went in constant fear of being blown up by mines. The new German pressure mines, called Oyster mines, were virtually unsweepable and took a steady toll of warships, freighters and landing craft.

In addition, the Germans sewed mines along the convoy routes and made determined night attacks on the Shuttle Service with E boats. These attacks were sustained for months. Most were beaten off by patrolling destroyers and MTB's but some broke through the screen and attacked the shipping with torpedoes.

LCTs were very difficult to sink with torpedoes because of their shallow draught and the way they had been constructed with compartmentalised double bottoms. They could take a tremendous amount of punishment before sinking. At least one E boat is said to have come to grief when it ran full tilt into the twelve tons of metal that formed the bow ramp of an LCT.

The greatest hazard to LCTs was the weather, which deteriorated after the invasion and which by 19th June had become a great storm. Over 800 major and minor landing craft were wrecked on the Normandy beaches in

50. Mark 4 LCTs launching DUKW's off the Normandy Beaches

two days, and the beaches became so cluttered with dangerous wrecks that arriving landing ships and craft were unable to unload or to beach in the huge waves. The Mulberry harbour in the American sector was wrecked and in the British sector it was damaged. In both cases the harbours were unable to accommodate all the shipping seeking shelter.

Some of the Mark 4 LCTs broke their backs on the way over to France in bad weather, tipping their heavy loads into the sea and drowning men in their vehicles. Many others strained their backs and had to be taken out of service so that they could be stiffened by welding railway lines to their bottoms and along their catwalks.

Immediately after the great storm, the landing craft Support Squadrons were formed into a single unit of about 70 Flak and Gun craft, to form, with a small number of Harbour Defence Motor Launches, HDML's, what was called the Support Squadron Eastern Flank, the SSEF. It was placed under the command of Commander K.A.Sellar, RN, who was known as 'Monkey' Sellar, previously the Force S Support Squadron Commander. It took over the task of inshore protection of the eastern flank from MTB's and minesweepers. At night the landing craft anchored several hundred yards apart in a single line known as the 'Trout' line, six miles long, mostly well within the range of the German shore batteries. By day the force dispersed to bombard the harrying German shore batteries. Night after night, for months, they protected the inshore waters of the eastern flank against German attacks, not without cost to themselves.

On 5th July the Germans launched an attack with 27 human torpedoes, that is, two torpedoes mounted one on top of the other. The top one was used as a cockpit for the driver who could fire the lower one. Four of them were destroyed but in the attack two of our minesweepers were sunk. Two nights later the Germans mounted an attack with 31 human torpedoes of which 15 were sunk. One of them was sunk by the commanding officer of an LCF using a Lewis gun to riddle the plastic dome of the attacking vessel, which was all that could be seen of it above the water. Afterwards he reported that he could clearly see the horror on the German sailor's face as he was being riddled with machine-gun bullets.

On August 3rd the Germans sent in wave after wave of explosive motor boats followed by 25 human torpedoes. The explosive motor boats were ten feet long and packed with explosives. They were either piloted or radio-controlled from piloted craft. The pilots jumped overboard once they had aligned their boats with a target. That night 32 explosive motor boats and the 25 human torpedoes were destroyed but not before they had sunk some shipping including a LCG(L).

On 9th August the Germans made another determined attack but this time the entire attacking force was either sunk or driven off and failed to sink any Allied shipping. Attacks on the eastern flank continued until the Germans were driven out of Le Havre on 12th September.

Among the victims of their persistent attacks was LCF 1, the unique mini-monitor which had moored in the Beaulieu river after the Dieppe raid. It blew up on 17th August, with very few survivors among its crew of nearly seventy. There are two versions of how it met its fate. One says it was torpedoed; the other says it had just sunk an explosive motor boat but that the latter exploded under the mini-monitor, detonating the ammunition in its magazines. Whatever the truth, she suffered the fate of several of the Gun and Flak craft which had very little protection round their magazines.

CHAPTER 7
WESTKAPELLE - THE JAWS OF DEATH

British naval casualties during the invasion had been astonishingly light. The plans had allowed for a loss of 10% of the landing craft and a further 20% damaged. There had been nowhere near these losses and the great storm of 19th June had sunk and damaged far more landing craft, especially minor landing craft of the Ferry Units, than had the enemy.

In terms of personnel, there had been far fewer casualties than had been anticipated and replacement crews were kicking their heels in holding camps at Mastodon at Exbury, Squid in Southampton, Tormentor at Bursledon and elsewhere.

The capture of the Cherbourg Peninsula by the Americans in June had removed much of the German naval threat to the western flank of the invasion beaches. But the eastern flank remained vulnerable until the capture of Le Havre in September, which meant that the defence of the eastern flank had to continue for three months. Clearly the same ships, coastal craft and landing craft could not withstand the strain of continuous night battles for such a long period. They had to be replaced from time to time. Both men and vessels suffered fatigue.

The Support craft began returning from Normandy at the end of June. The first craft to come back to the Beaulieu river were the Rocket craft which could serve no function other than beach assaults. LCT(R)s 438 and 460 were in and out of the river for a month before finally leaving never to return, paid off or sent to the Far East. While they were in the river they were joined by LCFs 26 and 36 and by LCG(L)s 2, 3, 13, 17, and 18, all formerly of G Force. Most of these Flak and Gun craft left after a week's respite. Some went north to pay off, some were sent for refits prior to sailing to the Far East and some went to local ports to await further action in Europe.

In mid-July LCG(L) 17 and LCF 36 returned and another batch of Support craft arrived for a rest. The newcomers were LCFs 19, 20, 32, and 38, and LCG(L)s 11, 680 and 764. The latter was sunk off Normandy a few weeks later. LCFs 32, 36, and 38, and LCG(L)s 2, 11, and 17 were destined to take part in the ferocious assault on Walcheren Island later in the autumn. Several of these craft had already survived the thick of the fighting in a series of contested assaults on the coasts of Sicily and Italy before returning to this country for the Normandy invasion.

LCG(L) 2, one of the oldest of the Gun craft, was commanded by a veteran officer, Lieutenant Arthur Cheney, RNVR, already the holder of two DSCs. He was soon to earn another. He can fairly be described as the most decorated RNVR officer ever to have sailed out of the Beaulieu river. He was about 30 years of age, 5 feet 8 inches in height, round faced, sandy haired and seemingly full of energy. A former acquaintance described him as an impressively efficient officer who had a habit of doing press-ups on his bridge when he came up to sniff the morning air. He had the reputation of being a very cool, determined and resourceful individual who would stubbornly keep his craft in action even while it was sinking beneath him. He had sailed to Dieppe from the Beaulieu river in TLC 126 which had been sunk during the raid. After Dieppe, he had taken command of LCF 18 and had sailed her to the Algerian port of Djidjelli to join a force of landing craft working up for the assault on Sicily, that is, Operation Husky. He saw much active service in the Mediterranean before returning to this country to take command of the old LCG(L) 2.

Towards the end of June, 12 American and 21 British LCVPs returned to the Beaulieu river. They were joined in September by 12 more LCVPs of the 813th Flotilla. The men from these craft, about 140 of them, British and American, are believed to have been accommodated in the Master Builder's House hotel, at Buckler's Hard.

By the beginning of September, large numbers of LCTs were returning to the Solent area, their task of cross-Channel ferrying no longer necessary now that ships could use the captured smaller ports.

In mid-September a steady stream of Mark 5 LCTs, all of them needing maintenance and repairs, moored in the Beaulieu river while awaiting attention or refits. Twenty different craft of the 102nd, 106th, 107th and 108th Flotillas came and went, some to return later, reassigned to the 102nd, 106th and 108th Flotillas which were based at Mastodon. By the end of September there were about twenty craft laying at the moorings, all of them veterans, all being held in reserve for further contingencies. All the craft of the 108th Flotilla, which had sailed from the river on D-Day as LCT(A), had now had their raised tank decks removed in local shipyards and reverted to being ordinary LCTs.

One interesting arrival at this time was LCT 3626, an American design Mark 6 LCT with ramps at both ends and with her superstructure divided down each side, allowing vehicles to drive through the craft in the fashion of the older Isle of Wight ferries that used to ply between Lymington and Yarmouth. It was somewhat larger than the Mark 5s and was manned by a British crew, a rarity for this type of craft which were very few in number and usually belonged to the U.S.Navy.

Throughout the late summer and the autumn, the Germans continued their strategy of denying the Allies the use of major ports like Cherbourg, Le Havre, Calais, Dunkirk and later, Antwerp. In all cases except Antwerp, they left a garrison of a division of soldiers to defend the ports until capture was inevitable, and then demolished them and rendered them useless for many months. This forced the Allies to continue to use the beachheads for longer than anticipated to shift huge quantities of supplies to their advancing armies. The great storm had demonstrated just how vulnerable this was to bad weather, and winter was approaching.

On 3rd September the Allies captured Antwerp intact, by-passing Dieppe, Calais, and Zeebrugge, but the Germans clung tenaciously to the north west coast of France and to the adjacent territories of Belgium and Holland. The port of Antwerp could not be used until the Germans had been cleared out of Holland and particularly out of the islands at the mouth of the shallow Scheldt estuary. The German stranglehold on the approaches to Antwerp denied the Allied armies the volume of supplies they needed to maintain the full momentum of their thrust towards the Ruhr, the heartland of German industry.

The autumn of 1944 saw some fearful land battles in the north west corner of Europe, including the futile British and Polish airborne assault on Arnhem on 17th September and the capture of what was left of Boulogne and Calais at the end of the same month. But the need for Antwerp remained and became imperative.

When Boulogne was captured the town and harbour were in ruins. The outer harbour was strewn with sunken wrecks and objects hazardous to shipping and was also sown with various types of mines. In the inner harbour, the jetties had been demolished either by Allied bombing or by the Germans who had also destroyed the gates to the inner basins which now dried out at low tide. No ships could be moored alongside any of the wharves because of the destruction and underwater obstructions and debris.

Early in October, six Mark 5 LCTs from the Beaulieu river were sent to Boulogne to ferry cargo from ships moored in the outer harbour or out at sea to the inner harbour where there was just one jetty remaining more or less intact along part of its length, sufficient to accommodate four LCTs.

But a German tank had been blown off the jetty into the water, and now lay with its gun pointing upwards like a solid metal stake, ready to puncture the engine room of the first LCT to tie above it. As the tide receded at a tremendous rate, (there was a 30ft rise and fall of the tide), the LCT duly squatted on the gun barrel, which put the craft out of action, permanently. It had to be towed away on the next tide and beached.

Wary of using the jetty thereafter, the remaining five craft sailed into an inner basin followed by a small French coaster. There was a 'ticker' mine in the basin entrance which allowed the five landing craft to pass over it before exploding under the French vessel which turned on to its side and sank in the basin entrance, bottling up the LCTs. As a result, six more Mark 5 LCTs sailed from the Beaulieu river to replace those rendered useless.

Among the six was LCT 2041 which had been the only LCT(A) of the 333rd Support Flotilla of J Force on D-Day. Now an ordinary LCT, she sailed with the other five out of Spithead one dark, cloudy, wet and windy night at the end of October, joining a convoy containing many of the Support craft that were destined to make the assault on Walcheren Island. Most of this convoy went to Ostend, but the six Mark 5s broke away during the night, heading for Boulogne, escorted by a solitary Harbour Defence Motor Launch.

They spent the next few months working the port, taking cargoes from the freighters moored offshore or in the outer harbour to the one and only usable jetty in the inner harbour, opposite the former German E boat pens, massively thick concrete structures that had been reduced to enormous slabs of rubble by RAF 'earthquake' bombs.

Soon after this group of LCTs started work, 2041 had a narrow escape from destruction. While unloading 90 tons of 40mm tank ammunition at the jetty at low spring tide, a German mine drifted in with the rising tide and exploded on a minute sandbank a few yards to seaward of 2041, lifting its stern well out of the water and showering it with seawater that descended from a column a hundred feet high. But for the little sandbank, which would have been covered in a few minutes by the fast rising tide, LCT 2041 would have been blown to pieces and the jetty would have been destroyed in the blast created by 90 tons of exploding ammunition.

The six craft working the port returned to the Beaulieu river for Christmas, leaving the original five to do the work after the entrance to the inner basin had been cleared of the wreck of the French freighter.

51. LCT 2041 on the beach at Normandy. Note the raised tank deck

The seaward approaches to the Belgium port of Antwerp is the Dutch waterway called the West Scheldt, and it was strewn with minefields and dominated from the north by Walcheren Island. There were over 30,000 German troops entrenched on the island in heavily fortified positions, well supplied with food, ammunition and fresh water. The island was defended by eighteen massive concrete batteries surrounded by land mines and by many other strong points, more than 100 guns, excluding anti-tank and anti-aircraft guns. All the ground surrounding the fortifications was below sea level, protected by a dyke. On the west coast was the small town of Westkapelle; on the south coast was Flushing and in the middle was the town of Middelburg. The east coast was joined to the mainland by a causeway from South Beveland, which was in Allied hands, as was the southern bank of the West Scheldt.

Planning for the assault on Walcheren Island, called Operation Infatuate, began in Ghent late in September. There was much discussion between Admiral Ramsey and his Navy, Army and Air Force advisers about how to subdue the massive shore batteries. The weather was becoming adverse for air and sea operations.

The Naval part of the operation was placed in the hands of Captain A.F.Pugsley, RN, the former J.1. Assault Group commander, of Lepe. Working in Ostend, he planned to land a force of Royal Marine Commandos at Westkapelle and a second force at Flushing from across the Scheldt from Breskens. Simultaneously, a third assault was to be made by a force of Canadian troops across the causeway linking the east of the island to the mainland.

The assault on Westkapelle was to be supported by the battleship HMS Warspite and by two monitors, HMS Erebus and HMS Roberts, to try to blast away the concrete fortifications. Because of the shallow water, inshore support could only be given by Support landing craft drawn from the Support Squadron Eastern Flank, the SSEF. In the event the batteries were found to be too formidable to be silenced by the ships and craft assigned to do the job, even with generous air support.

Of the seventy craft that had made up the SSEF on the Trout Line, thirty six were unserviceable. Only twenty five were available for the operation, comprising six Flak

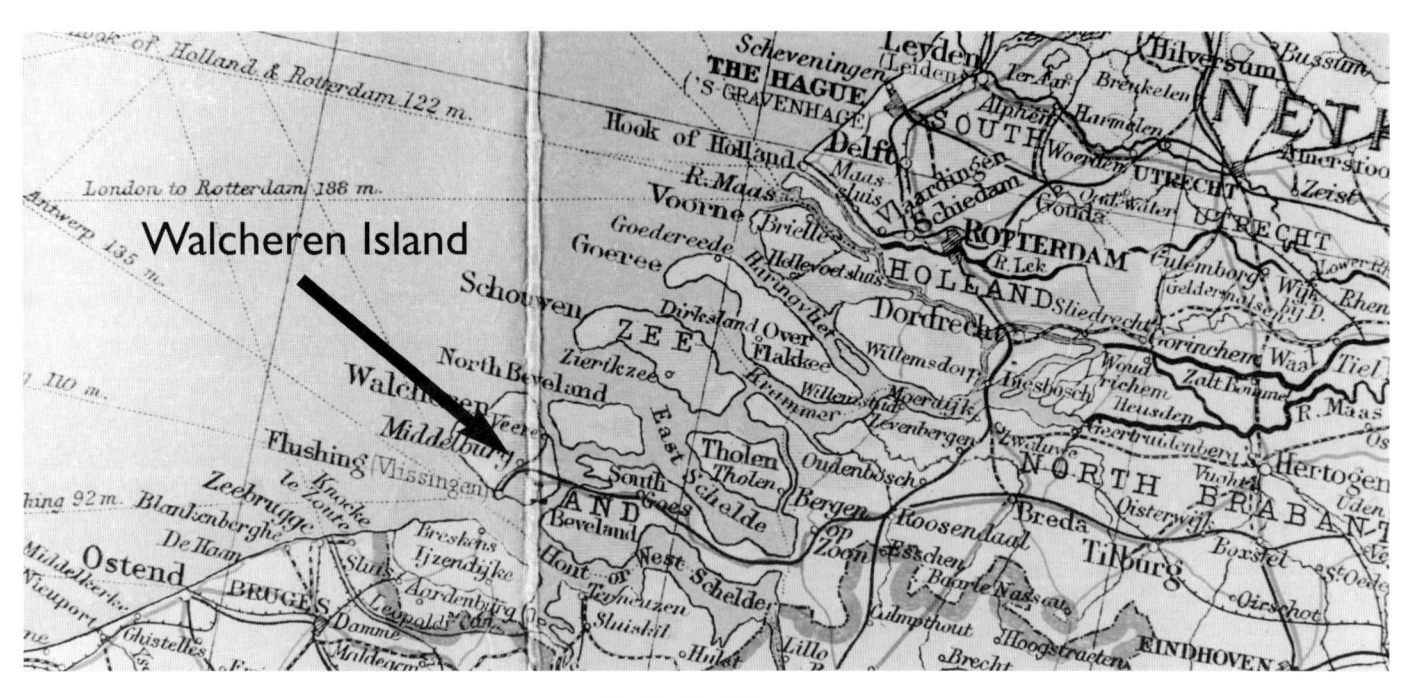

52. The Scheldt Eastuary

craft, six Gun craft and five Rocket craft. Three of the Flak craft and three of the Gun craft were selected from those that had rested in the Beaulieu river in July. They included LCG(L) 2 commanded by Lieutenant Arthur Cheney, RNVR.

53. Commander K. A. Sellar RN, who led the Support craft at Walcheren Island

Pugsley was to control the operation from the Headquarters ship, HMS Kingsmill and the Support Squadron was still under the command of Commander K.A.(Monkey) Sellar, RN, who would be sailing in LCH (Landing Craft Headquarters) 98. Many of the communications ratings for HMS Kingsmill and LCH 98 were drawn from Mastodon at Exbury for this operation, as were some of the Beach Signals units and RN Commando. The Beachmaster at Westkapelle was to be Commander R.M.(Smokey) Prior, RN, Pugsley's former Senior Staff Officer at Lepe.

The Mastodon contingents left Exbury on Monday 23rd October, and sailed with the main force to Ostend for rehearsals before the assault on 1st November.

Prior to the assault a large force of RAF bombers was used to breach the dykes in four places round the rim of the island, flooding it to impede German troop and supply movements; it also impeded the movement of our own troops after the assault. Over two hundred bombers were then used before the assault in an attempt to subdue the concrete gun emplacements and batteries, but with only limited success.

The weather on November 1st was foul, with low clouds, rain and fog. The assault force of infantry and tank landing craft escorted by the Flak, Gun and Rocket craft, arrived off Westkapelle at 7 a.m. The sea was strewn with minefields and the weather was so thick that navigation off the featureless coast was very difficult. Because of the weather the spotter aircraft directing the shellfire of the Warspite, Erebus and Roberts could not see the fall of shot, and the supporting fighter-bombers were unable to see their targets.

Sellar had briefed his Support craft to draw the fire of the shore batteries on to themselves to enable the infantry and tank landing craft to sneak in to the beaches before the Germans realised what was happening. He was taking advantage of the Germans' habit of being unable to resist shooting back at anything that shot at them, even if it was with peashooters like the Flak crafts' little 20mm Oerlikon guns and their 2-pounder pom-poms. Not even the 4.7 inch guns of the six Gun craft could do more than chip bits of concrete off the massive gun emplacements. But while the German guns were duelling with the Support craft they were not firing at the tank and infantry landing craft thereby allowing the commandos and their guns and vehicles to get ashore relatively unscathed.

Under a torrent of heavy shell fire, the Support craft moved in to point blank range to worry the heavy shore batteries. Three of the five Rocket craft in the formation were hit without blowing up; one was struck seven times and remained afloat. Unfortunately the rockets of one of them fell among our own landing craft.

Of the craft that had lain in the Beaulieu river, LCF 36, after previously being hit by our own rockets, was sunk by enemy gunfire. LCF 38 was also hit by enemy shell fire, caught fire and after surviving members of her crew had been taken off by another craft she blew up. LCF 32 and LCG(L)s 11 and 17 were badly damaged.

LCG(L) 2, Cheney's craft, was sunk after sustaining a spectacular amount of damage. It had been engaging the German guns at close range for some time when our own rockets fell on her, killing and injuring members of her crew. As a survivor said afterwards, the craft was enshrouded in a pall of black smoke and the blasting effect of the rockets exploding on the craft made it feel as though it was being hammered into the sea with giant metal tent pegs. Cheney took evasive action to get out of the rockets' line of fire, and then returned to the business of shelling the enemy shore batteries. Eventually LCG(L) 2 was hit in the engine room. Cheney ordered the flooding engine room to be abandoned with the engines running, (as he had also done at Dieppe), and steamed out to sea still firing his guns. When the flooded engines stopped, the craft continued firing until the tide swung the craft to a position which prevented her from bringing her guns to bear. At this point, Sellar's LCH, itself riddled with shells and shrapnel, pulled alongside and pushed Cheney's craft round so that it could continue firing, but both craft came under heavy and accurate enemy gunfire which caused more damage and casualties to the helpless, immobile LCG(L) 2. Then a very brave young commanding officer of LCT 789, which had successfully discharged its cargo, passed a tow rope to the

54. Landing craft H.Q. used to control assault landings

crippled Gun craft, but shortly afterwards both craft struck mines. As they struggled with the damage, LCG(L) 2 was struck by another mine, and this time the craft rolled over and sank.

Of the thirty three Royal Marines she had in her crew, only four remained alive and uninjured; the rest were killed, drowned or badly injured. Miraculously, there were only two casualties among the naval members of her crew. Cheney survived and was subsequently awarded his third Distinguished Service Cross, and other members of his crew were decorated.

Among the craft that had fought to the finish and had been sunk were two Gun craft of a brand new design, Landing Craft Gun (Medium), or LCG(M), 101 and 102, both of which suffered dreadful casualties. Three other craft of a similar size, the Landing Craft Support (Large), LCS(L)s, which had wooden hulls and looked like torpedo boats but with much heavier guns on their fore decks, were burning wrecks and had to be abandoned.

The Support craft suffered appalling casualties from the German guns. Of the twenty five craft that had engaged the defences, nine were sunk and eleven were badly damaged, i.e. 80% became casualties. One hundred and ninety two officers and men were killed and a further 126 were severely wounded.

Just after 11 a.m., their work done, what remained of the Support Squadron limped back towards Ostend. At half past two the next afternoon Commander K.A.Sellar sent the following signal to the survivors of his Squadron:-

> "I cannot express to the officers and men of the remnants of our Squadron my pride and admiration in you and your lost shipmates. You held the key to the speedy end of the war against Germany and you turned it with the utmost determination and courage. Those we have left behind remain a memorial to the Support Squadron Eastern Flank."

It says much for their sacrifice that only one tank landing craft was sunk during the assault.

After the assault landing, it took the British and Canadian forces seven days to capture the island. Following its capture it was discovered that not one of the German batteries had been silenced or even seriously damaged by the Support craft. The latters' puny fire power had been like trying to shatter a milk bottle by blowing rice at it through a straw. The commandos and the RAF had to subdue the batteries by land and air attacks.

It took another three weeks to clear the West Scheldt of mines before the port of Antwerp could be opened. In the meantime more Support craft sailed from Britain to fight the German Navy's frogmen, human torpedoes, explosive motor boats and mines among the islands and shallow waterways of the East Scheldt. And the Support craft endured further difficult assaults on Schouwen and other islands to the north of Walcheren.

Back in Britain, in the wardrooms of Mastodon at Exbury, Squid in Southampton and other landing craft

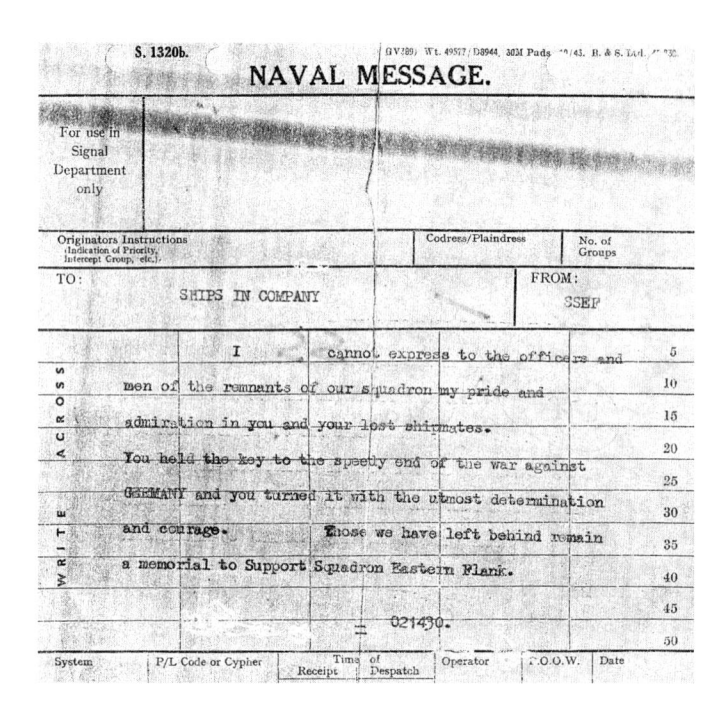

55. The original signal from SSEF

bases in the Solent area, Captain A.F.Pugsley acquired the sobriquet "Bloody" for the casualties that had been sustained by the tactics adopted at Westkapelle. Few of his junior RNVR officers understood why the Support Squadron had been used as a turkey shoot for the Germans instead of supplying an adequate bombarding force of capital ships to distract or silence the shore batteries.

During the rest of the winter, which was exceptionally cold that year, the Allied armies suffered a series of reverses. The German defensive successes at Arnhem, Aachen and Antwerp were followed by their nearly successful Ardennes offensive late in December which broke through the Allied front into Belgium and threatened to re-occupy Antwerp. It was not contained until 27th December, after very bitter fighting over the

Christmas period. It was Hitler's last attempt to stem the Allied advance into Germany from the west.

There was no further necessity for assaults from the sea in north west Europe and consequently there was no further role for Combined Operations in this theatre. Already attention had been switched to the Far East. In fact soon after the Normandy landings the American landing ships started leaving Europe for the Pacific.

By Christmas 1944 the British landing craft fleet had virtually ceased ferrying men and materials across the Channel, replaced by cargo vessels. The assault landing ships had reverted to being ordinary troop ships, having long since discharged their assault landing craft, the LCAs, and their crews, and replaced the craft with ordinary life boats. The tank and infantry landing craft were being sent in droves to shipyards all round the country and to Northern Ireland to be 'tropicalised' for service in the Far East. The first craft to be taken out of service were the Rocket craft, followed by other Support craft. The older tank landing craft were being scrapped and superceded by a new version of the Mark 4 LCT, redesigned for ocean passages and for service in the tropics.

Several of the Mark 5 LCTs from the Beaulieu river had already gone for tropical refits and were later to be lifted on to the decks of tank landing ships at Portsmouth for passage to HMS Chinkara, the landing craft base on the Cochin river in south west India. By Christmas there were no more than a dozen Mark 5s on the moorings, manned by skeleton crews, the majority of the officers and men having been sent on shore leave, which for many of them was the last leave they would get before sailing to the Far East.

Mastodon was being run down at a rapid rate. The G and J Force planning staffs of Naval and WRNS officers and Wrens had long gone. Many of the WRNS officers were sent to naval headquarters in north west Europe or had been shipped to India and Ceylon. Nevertheless, contemporary photographs show that there were at least sixty seven Wrens, including their officers, at Mastodon in the early months of 1945, and they were still housed in the Montagu Arms hotel at Beaulieu.

Exbury was still in use for transient parties of naval officers and ratings, especially communication ratings who were being formed into units of about sixty. They were being kitted out with khaki battledress and shipped across to Germany and elsewhere to perform unspecified duties under such titles as Naval Party 1734 and Naval Party 1740. One of these two units finished up at Kiel.

Probably the very last operation carried out by landing craft from the Beaulieu river was a mission of mercy to devasted Holland, where the population was on the verge of starvation. Craft from the 102nd and 108th Flotillas of Mark 5 LCTs left the river in March and sailed for Flushing, the scene of bitter fighting during the assault on Walcheren Island, to ferry supplies in these shallow waterways. From here they moved south across the West Scheldt to the small town of Terneuzen and thence to a smaller town on the canal to Ghent where they remained until V.E. Day. Afterwards they were used to carry German prisoners of war from Holland back to Germany.

The Wrens from Mastodon and many of the male members of the ship's company turned out in force to watch the flotillas of Mark 5s sail for Holland. They were probably the very last major landing craft to use the Beaulieu river, and their flotilla staff were the last flotilla staff to be based at Exbury. This was barely two months before the end of the war in Europe where hostilities ceased on the night of 8th May 1945.

CHAPTER 8
FORTUNES OF WAR

Nothing is more irritating to the wartime generation than a younger generation of historians, novelists and especially T.V. scriptwriters, attempting to recapture the life and times of the second world war. They nearly always get something wrong, like using modern speech habits or slang in their dialogue, or using modern social habits or the wrong culture patterns, or giving characters a freedom of action or movement that simply was not possible during the war.

By today's standards people suffered immense restrictions, shortages and stress, endured unbelievable hardships and danger, and bore it all with staggering equanimity, even accepting the dreadful waste of life as a commonplace fact of war. Nevertheless, there was a selfless unity of purpose and social cohesion driven by common adversity which is so absent today in our grasping, shiftless society. In wartime, people helped each other unstintingly in the certain knowledge that they might themselves need help by the end of the day. People who exploited the misfortunes of others were hounded and socially ostracised or could be sent to prison for contravening one of the many wartime regulations governing day to day behaviour.

Everybody lived perpetually on the brink of personal and national catastrophe, and actual catastrophe overtook a high percentage of the population in the form of homes destroyed by bombing, families broken up and scattered across the world, close relatives killed or severely wounded, or made prisoner of war.

Death and injury through enemy action was never very far away for any member of the population, whether service or civilian, unless they lived in remote areas of Wales or Scotland, beyond the reach of the Luftwaffe and the flying bombs and rockets which came over the south coast in droves soon after D-Day.

The flying bombs, nicknamed 'doodlebugs', like the Cruise Missiles fired at Bagdad during the Gulf War, presented the anti-aircraft defences with a terrible dilemma. Unless they were blown up in mid-air, there was no way of controlling where they fell. And when they fell, the one ton of explosives that they carried detonated on impact, killing and injuring people indiscriminately. It was a terrifying weapon which snatched at and held the attention of everybody within earshot with the ugly snarl of its engine. Conversation ceased and there was an ominous silence while everybody listened intently for its engine to cut out, the signal that it had begun its glide to earth. Then everybody ran for cover and waited for the explosion. Nobody ever got used to it, but they learned to live with it just the same, even though the 'doodlebugs' came over many times a day at one period.

Southampton and the surrounding area received its share of them and one fell on the west bank of the Beaulieu river. The blast was felt at Beaulieu and Exbury. One also fell on the small-arms ammunition dump at HMS Tormenter at Bursledon and another fell on a nearby ATS (later called the Womens' Royal Army Corps), officers' mess killing and injuring all the women in the building.

In addition to the ever present threat of death from enemy action there was a laxity with safety precautions that would scandalise the modern generation. For example, there was no special protection round the magazines of the Flak, Gun and Rocket craft, which for their size carried huge amounts of ammunition, 100,000 rounds in the case of the Flak craft and over 2,000 heavy rockets in the case of the LCT(R). Most of the Coastal Forces craft and many of the major landing craft of a similar size were made of wood and carried thousands of gallons of high octane petrol in tanks that had no special protection and which exploded into horrific infernos when they were hit by enemy shell fire. Another example is that all hot pipes in HM ships were lagged with asbestos.

A very large number of service and civilian personnel were handling explosives, in factories, on the railways, in warehouses and at ammunition dumps. Live ammunition was in daily use by the services for routine elementary training purposes. Fatal accidents were commonplace. During the preparation for the Dieppe raid a commando accidentally set off a hand grenade in the crowded confines of a troopdeck of the landing ship HMS Invicta, killing and injuring twenty five men.

Almost every rehearsal for combat produced a crop of fatal accidents. One, mentioned by Nevil Shute in 'Requiem for a Wren', occurred when a soldier drowned after his tank toppled off the ramp of an LCT into a deep water hole in the beach at Newtown on the Isle of Wight. The hole had been created by the screws of another LCT that had used the same spot for kedging off.

There were also many accidents that would today be described as 'industrial'. A naval rating set himself alight and burned like a blowtorch while foolishly attempting to dispose of unwanted confidential books by burning them in a bucket of petrol on the tank deck of an LCT at a hard at Northam. In an incident at a small Northam shipyard, a drunken sailor returning from a night ashore fell into an empty dry dock that had no guard rails round it, and sustained severe head injuries and broken limbs.

Throughout the war the crews of many minor and major landing craft were drowned during bad weather. The number of men who were drowned when their minor landing craft and barges were swamped in the Channel on D-Day will never be known but must have been substantial. The same applies to those who were drowned by the great storm on 19th June. In one terrible incident earlier in the war, nearly two hundred officers and ratings were drowned when 18 LCTs foundered in bad weather en route to the Mediterranean. In another incident, two brand new LCG(L)s, Nos. 15 and 16, were swamped and foundered off Milford Haven, due to a design fault, and nearly one hundred officers, ratings and marines were drowned.

With death, injury, bereavement and stress so near to hand, almost everybody drove themselves to live life to the full, as if there would be no tomorrow.

Everybody worked excessively long hours, so much so that productivity in factories went down instead of up in relation to the hours worked, because of fatigue. A great many of the men and women who worked in the auxiliary services like the ARP or the Fire Service, or in factories or upon the land, did additional part time war work of some sort. Those who worked by day in shops and offices joined such organisations as the Home Guard or the Observer Corps, or worked as part-time nursing auxiliaries, ambulance drivers, fire-watchers or for one of the other emergency services. Very many joined voluntary welfare organisations producing food, clothing and other necessities for those who had been bombed out or were otherwise in need of material help or comfort. There were very few people whose work or leisure activities were not connected with the war effort.

A huge proportion of the male population between the ages of 18 and 51 had been conscripted into the armed services or directed into essential war work, though some had to be left in "Reserved" occupations such as senior civil servants, code-breakers, and scientists, artisans and technicians doing essential manufacturing, or maintenance of railways and power stations, and those concerned with food production and distribution. Even the elderly and the unfit were often doing essential war work, as, for example, many of the thousands of labourers and carpenters employed on building components of the Mulberry harbour.

Women replaced conscripted men in an enormous variety of skilled, semi-skilled and unskilled occupations, in factories, in local government, in banking and commerce, in running the transport system, and a host of other essential jobs. The nations communications networks must have been almost entirely run by women as were nursing and associated rehabilitation and welfare services. And of course, a large proportion of young unmarried women joined one of the three womens' branches of the armed services.

One of the interesting demographic features of the war is that a high proportion of the men and women in the armed services were remarkably young, and their promotion to positions of heavy responsibility was often rapid. One had to register for military service at 17 years of age and was conscripted or could volunteer for active service at 18. Between the ages of 17 and 18 one was compelled to do some sort of 'voluntary' war service, like fire-watching. By the age of 20 they were veterans, if they were still alive, and many had been promoted to NCOs or officers. Many of the regular officers were relatively young for their ranks. Captain A.F.Pugsley was promoted to that rank at the age of 42, (compared to Swinley who did not attain that rank until he was about 50) and R.E.D. Ryder, V.C. was already a Commander at the age of 34.

A high proportion of the commanding officers of major landing craft were in their mid-twenties and held the rank of Lieutenant or Sub-Lieutenant in the RNVR. Sub-Lieutenant commanding officers were commonplace, to the puzzlement of the army and the RAF, where rank went with command. The 1st Lieutenants of major landing craft were usually between 20 and 22 years of age; the younger were Midshipmen and the older were Sub-Lieutenants, the latter often of the same rank as their commanding officers, which was very confusing for their army passengers.

These very young men were given crushing responsibilities. They were made wholly responsible, in the traditional Navy fashion, for their 500 ton vessels and all who sailed in them, in fair weather or foul, in formation or alone, in port or at sea, under attack from enemy aircraft, surface vessels and submarines and exposed to underwater hazards like drifting, moored or oyster mines. It has been said that no other Service placed so much responsibility on so many young officers as did the Navy. And they acquitted themselves extremely well, as exemplified in the assault on Walcheren Island.

By today's standards almost everybody was relatively poorly paid. The basic pay of a naval rating of the rank of Able Seaman was three shillings a day, or, in new decimal money, £1.05p a week. A Wren received 1 shilling and 4 pence a day, less than 50p in new money, per week. A male Petty Officer earned 2 guineas (£2.10p new money) a week and a Wren P.O. a miserly £1-8s-0d, (£1.40p). A Midshipman, the lowest rank of commissioned naval officer, received £2-7s-8d (£2.37p) a week, less than a 3rd Officer in the WRNS, who received just over £3, which was two thirds of the pay of her male equivalent, a Sub-Lieutenant, who was paid £4-10s-1d (£4.50p). All the male naval officers received extra allowances, like command money if they commanded a major landing craft, and all members of major landing craft crews were paid 'hard lying' money to compensate them for their primitive living conditions. For a Sub-Lieutenant this was 1s-6d a day, or 50p a week in new money.

Four-ringed Captains, such as Swinley and Pugsley received a basic pay of £28-6s-4d a week, i.e. £1,471 per annum, plus numerous allowances including Command Money.

Many of the servicemen who had been conscripted from salaried and superannuated occupations were also entitled to the 'balance of civil pay' if their service pay was less than they received in their civilian jobs. These men were relatively wealthy compared with their compatriots of the same rank who had to make do with their service pay.

All ranks were fed free of charge, but officers received additional mess bills for some of their food, and bar bills for their drinks. Ratings received a free tot of rum each day. Wrens did not receive this dubious privilege.

Living conditions for the men, and to a lesser extent the women of the armed services, were often crude to rough, and downright primitive by today's standards. The men on active service with the Ferry Units lived rough in their small landing craft and barges, only marginally better off than the men of the various beach units living under their individual ground sheets in holes in the beach or in the ground.

In temporary barracks such as those at Exbury, the huts were dormitories, unheated for most of the time because of the scarcity of fuel, and without toilet facilities. These were in nearby unheated ablution blocks, containing toilets round the outside, a row of handbasins down the middle and perhaps a couple of baths in one corner, all very well ventilated. Hot water and soap were scarce.

Afloat, keeping clean was a major problem. Unlike the American-built Infantry landing craft, the LCI(L)s, which had reasonable washrooms and showers, living conditions on British LCTs and the Support craft variants were only marginally better than those of the Ferry Units. The officers shared a handbasin in a cubbyhole of a toilet off the wardroom. The absence of baths was keenly felt and many officers from the major landing craft in Southampton Water went ashore to the Dolphin and the Star hotels, Below Bar, with a towel and a bar of soap stuffed up their monkey jackets and sneaked upstairs for a surreptitious hot bath in one of the hotels' bathrooms. The ratings, perhaps forty of them in the Support craft, had nowhere else to go and shared an inadequate number of washbasins and toilets in the wet and windy fo'c'sle of their craft.

Complaints from the officers or the men of the landing craft crews about their living conditions met with the retort "You're a damned sight better off than the men in the army!"

The sailors did their dhobying in the traditional Nelson fashion, in a bucket of hot water on deck and then had problems drying their clothes; lines of drying washing were never encouraged on British warships.

The officers sent their clothes ashore to local laundries, numerous in those days, and had particular difficulties getting their detachable starched collars laundered. These could be boxed and sent through the post to specialised collar laundries. It meant that officers were obliged to keep considerable stocks of clean white shirts and collars to tide them over periods away from home ports.

In those days refrigerators were rare and none of the smaller vessels possessed one. The diet comprised mainly dried and tinned foods. Fresh bread and fresh vegetables, when available, had to be replenished at frequent intervals. Store parties came ashore from the landing craft every three or four days. If a craft was on active service the crew had to make do with 'compo' rations, the same as the army. But unlike the army or the sailors in larger vessels, the landing craft crews were not fed by professional cooks. The cook in a landing craft was a member of the crew, often one who'd had his arm twisted to get him to 'volunteer' for the job, and he was paid an extra three pence a day for the privilege of being in a position to devastate the digestions of his shipmates.

The galleys in landing craft were often in a niche of the cramped messdeck, where the extra heat was welcome but where the smells of cooking and the noise of clattering pots were not, to the men trying to sleep after a night watch.

In view of the long hours that people worked and the stresses and strains of war, it is not surprising that many indulged themselves with excessive smoking and drinking and plunged with relish into every opportunity for partying and dancing and into every form of entertainment.

The service men and women were so poorly paid that they could not often afford a visit to the fleshpots of nearby cities such as Southampton, where there was a Nuffield Club and a NAAFI Club, which were recreational centres that provided seemingly luxurious facilities like decent lounges, writing rooms, first class entertainment and dancing to a full orchestra.

The social life of every camp site and barrack area was often rich, hectic and diverse by today's standards where the television set and television programmes dominate leisure hours. The service personnel themselves organised an incredible variety of entertainments. Drawn from all walks of life, there was nearly always somebody who could play an instrument or who was prepared to sing a sentimental popular song of the period or organise a concert.

In isolated spots like Exbury they had to make their own amusements although like most camps there was a cinema for both recreational and training purposes. But dances and entertainment were arranged at the Domus at Beaulieu, or in the village hall at Exbury, or, on a smaller scale, in the Wrens' quarters at the Montagu Arms hotel, where there was usually a party every month. Many small camps, if they were lucky, received occasional visits from a small company of professional performers from the ENSA organisation.

The local civilian population, especially the women, always did their bit to provide recreational facilities for the troops, despite the severe rationing and oppressive restrictions on just about everything we take so much for granted today.

Yet there was one luxury that was exceedingly hard to come by, the luxury of being alone, to get away from the unrelenting communal existence of camp, barrack and shipboard life.

In those days it was exceedingly difficult for civilians and service personnel to wander very far from their homes and bases. Few civilians possessed cars and those who did were unable to obtain petrol unless their cars were used for essential business or for purposes related to the war effort. Public transport was scarce.

The services had ample transport for duty purposes but it was limited for recreational trips into towns and local centres of entertainment. Consequently hitch-hiking on duty transport was commonplace, and it says much for the moral standards of those days that young service women could hitch a lift without fear of being molested.

However, except for travel on main roads, there were very severe restrictions on peoples' movements. Whole areas were declared out of bounds and if one strayed into them one ran the risk of being arrested, punished or, in some cases, shot by a sentry. The areas around Beaulieu and Exbury were subjected to particularly severe movement restrictions because of the secrecy surrounding many of the activities taking place in the locality, such as the Special Operations Executive's 'Finishing School' for secret agents, the French secret agents' centre at Inchmery, and the construction sites for the pieces of the Mulberry harbour.

Undue curiosity aroused great suspicion and penalties. All service personnel were impelled to curb their curiosity with the slogan "Careless Talk Costs Lives". People simply did not enquire too closely into what other people were doing, with the result that they led very insular lives. For instance, most of the Wrens on the staff at Mastodon had no idea of the nature of the duties of the men and women of the many and diverse units that stayed there before moving on, or what was happening on the opposite bank of the Beaulieu river. They were too busy with their own duties, working excessively long hours during the preparations for D-Day, although afterwards they could relax a little, if their officers would let them. For much of the time all ranks were forbidden to wander about Exbury Gardens, not just to prevent them from picking rare blooms, spoiling the gardens or courting but also because of the secrecy surrounding naval and military usages of the site.

Mastodon's ship's routine could be made as irksome as Captain Swinley and his 1st Lieutenant, Lieutenant-Commander C.R.Clark, RN, a brash and bulky Antipodean, deemed necessary. By all accounts, Swinley was a stickler for traditional naval routines and discipline, and gave his officers, including the WRNS officers, a particularly hard time. It was not the happiest of wardrooms, (officers' mess). He seems to have been grossly inconsiderate of his subordinates. There is a story that he kept his Royal Marine orderly on duty day and night until the man collapsed with fatigue and was removed to the sick bay. Several sources stated that he kept the wardroom bar open and its stewards on duty until it suited him to order it to close, often far into the night, and expected the stewards to be on duty at the normal time the following day. He is said to have compelled his senior officers, Commanders and Lieutenant-Commanders, to report to him every time they wished to leave the premises.

There are also reports of him prowling round Exbury House in the dead of night, presumably to ensure that the night staff were awake, and of the duty Regulating Petty Officer phoning round the offices where the Wrens were alone on duty so that they could lock their doors if they wished to do so. Swinley and his wife rented a house somewhere in the locality and he did not spend every night at Exbury House. But when he did, everybody was on the alert.

Everybody, men and women, officers and ratings, seem to have been very wary of him. Some hated him so much that, according to several different sources, his pet Great Dane by the name of Jeeves was poisoned out of spite. This may have been rumour because several other people reported that the dog was very much alive and took part in a dog race for the pets of the ship's company during a garden fete in the grounds of Exbury House on August Bank Holiday, 1944.

There are many stories of his distaste for Wrens and of punishments meted out to them for petty infractions. A Wren who had the temerity to make a social visit to one of the major landing craft suffered a week's loss of pay and a month's confinement to barracks. An entire group of Wren trot boat crews were harshly punished for getting tiddly on a bottle of gin while off duty.

But not all the stories about him were adverse. On one occasion Supply Wren Joan Firth, aged 20, ignored the call to 'rise and shine' at 6.30 one morning, fell asleep, missed breakfast at 7 a.m. and also the transport from the Montagu Arms to Exbury at 7.30. She managed to hitch a lift from Beaulieu to Hilltop, and started the three mile walk from there to Exbury. Having forfeited breakfast she was hungry and picked a hatfull of juicy blackberries so that she could eat while she walked. She heard a car approach and stood in the road to stop it and hitch a lift. To her surprise and consternation, the passenger was Captain Swinley on his way to work. She jammed her hat on her head, blackberries and all, snapped to attention and saluted. He told her to get into the car and they drove in complete silence to Exbury. The sentry on the main gate nearly dropped his rifle while trying to salute when he saw a grinning young Wren sitting with the Captain at that hour of the morning! She alighted inside the gates and never heard another word about the escapade and only later became aware of the speculation circulating in the Regulating Office, a hotbed of surmise, gossip and rumour.

Despite the tyrannies that Swinley seems to have inflicted on his officers and ratings, the Wrens of the ship's company and some of the ratings regarded Mastodon as a particularly happy ship to serve in and look back on their time at Exbury with fondness and pleasure. The Wrens seem to have been very well looked after at the Montagu Arms hotel which was particularly well run by WRNS 3rd Officer P.M.Irvine. She was evidently popular.

For most of the young Wrens, the war was a great, liberating, experience that allowed them to get away from the social and other constraints of a dull home life in the days when most women lived with their parents until they married. Similarly, very many of those who worked before the war were restricted to a limited range of secretarial and clerical jobs or jobs as shop assistants or telephonists or in catering or in dismal demeaning manual occupations in factories. Few enjoyed a higher education that led to professional status. But the second world war had, as in the first, provided untold opportunities for women to enter into an enormous variety of jobs formerly done by men, and gave them a freedom of choice and action and chances of promotion that women of today take for granted as a right. They could become mechanics and fitters, signallers, radio and radar operators, and all manner of engineering, non-engineering and operative jobs in addition to the traditional womens' occupations, and they could rise to senior executive and administrative positions.

One of the more unusual and strenuous tasks undertaken by the Wrens was that of small boats' crews. The Mastodon trot boat crews worked on the Beaulieu river in all weathers, at all hours of the day and night, whenever a boat was needed to haul an LCT off the mudflats, or take carousing sailors back to their landing craft, or senior officers down to Lepe and sometimes further into the Solent. They helped the perpetual store parties to load and unload heavy sacks of food and

56. The Wrens of HMS Mastodon, 1945

57. Petty officer Sue Cavendish WRNS, Mastodon trot boat cox'n

equipment into and out of the trot boats and assisted drunken sailors and officers to get back safely to their craft, across slippery decks. Most of these Wrens were barely out of their teens and some of the Wren Petty Officer cox'ns were little more than twenty. One of the latter, Sue Cavendish, the tall and elegant daughter of a RNVR Captain, who had joined up at the age of 17, had the distinction at the end of the war of being present with her crew at the surrender of a German U Boat (submarine), the U 249, as it approached Portland harbour.

When the war in Europe ended on 8th May 1945, so did the need for Combined Operations bases in the Solent area. Shortly after VE Day, Captain Pugsley, Commander Sellar and the survivors of the Support Squadron Eastern Flank, now renamed T Force, met in Romsey for a raucous farewell party at the White Horse hotel.

The exodus from Mastodon had begun at the end of March and by the beginning of April most of the ratings and Wrens had gone and the Wrens quarters in the Montagu Arms hotel had closed. A small care and maintenance party of ratings and Wrens was left at Exbury House and by the end of May the senior WRNS officer of Mastodon, 2nd Officer N.M.Dudley, and two Wren Regulating Petty Officers, Vera Miller and Betty Thompson, witnessed the last of the Exbury Wrens climb tearfully into a lorry and drive away, drafted elsewhere. Soon afterwards the two RPO's were themselves seen into a three-ton lorry by 2nd Officer Dudley, "just the two of us" wrote Vera Miller, "in that big transport, and all weepy, too."

On 6th July 1945, HMS Mastodon paid off, although Exbury House remained requisitioned by the Navy. Just over a month later, on 14th August, Japan surrendered and the second world war came to an end.

Gone forever were the seven thousand men who had manned the landing craft and the senior officers who had commanded them from Exbury House and Lepe House.

Captain Pugsley rose to the rank of Rear Admiral. He died in July 1990 at the age of 88. Captain Swinley and Commander Sellar returned to retirement. Commander Ryder, V.C. was promoted to the rank of Captain. He died in 1986 at the age of 78. He and Commodore Hughes-Hallett, who rose to the rank of Vice Admiral, became Members of Parliament after the war. Hughes-Hallett died in 1972 at the relatively early age of 71. He had left Combined Operations, which he had helped to father, in December 1943 to take command of the cruiser HMS Jamaica. Soon afterwards Jamaica played a major part in sinking the German battle cruiser Scharnhorst.

Their overall commander, Admiral Sir Bertram Ramsey never lived to reap the rewards of his triumphs at Dunkirk and Normandy. He was killed in an air crash while taking off from a Paris airport on 2nd January 1945.

Gone forever were the thousands of landing craft that had swarmed into the Solent and Southampton Water, into the Hamble, the Itchen and the Beaulieu rivers, and into the creeks and rivers along the north shores of the Isle of Wight.

Many of the craft from these waters had already been dispatched to the Far East to take part in Operation Zipper, the assault on Malaya. The assault force of over 300 vessels included a Support Squadron of ten Rocket craft and seven Gun craft, a squadron of thirty eight Infantry landing craft and over one hundred LCTs. They had left their bases in India and sailed nearly 2,000 miles across the Bay of Bengal and the Andaman sea to the Malaya peninsula, a fantastic feat for the major landing craft. But Japan surrendered just before the force arrived and the 65,000 British and Indian troops were used to re-occupy Malaya and Singapore.

Some of the LCIs and Gun craft from the assault force were used to rescue Dutch citizens from the East Indies during the savage little war of independence which the Indonesians waged against the Dutch.

Six LCI(L)s of a follow-up squadron sailed under their own steam as far east as Hong Kong, but upon their arrival in March 1946 they were paid off after a couple of forays against Chinese pirates and brief use for carrying fresh water in their double-bottom tanks to outlying islands suffering severe drought. They were later returned to the U.S. Navy base at Port Olongopo in Subic Bay in Luzon and abandoned in the huge graveyard of unwanted U.S. warships.

A large number of major landing craft of all types lay in rivers and ports all along the route from Plymouth to the Far East, wherever they happened to be when the war with Japan ended.

Many of the Mark 5 LCTs that had sailed from the Beaulieu river for tropical refits in the winter of 1944 were, in October 1945, lying in creeks off Malabar

Island, near Cochin, on the south west coast of India. One or two were sold to local companies but the majority were broken up or ended their days ignominiously by being scuttled in the Indian Ocean. They were Lease-Lend material, and under the terms on which they had been supplied to Britain they had to be returned to the United States or scrapped. It was too expensive and impractical to sail them back to America, and they were unwanted by the U.S. Navy bases in South East Asia. So, along with thousands of Jeeps and warplanes, many of them brand new, they were scrapped or dumped into the Indian Ocean.

Back at home, many of the landing craft left in the Solent area ended their days in scrap yards in Southampton and Portsmouth. One of the biggest of the local scrap yards for LCTs lay alongside Northam bridge on the eastern bank of the river Itchen, and many of the rusting hulks were still there in the early 1960's. The remains of one modified LCT lay in a scrapyard alongside the M275 at Portsea until the scrapyard was cleared in the late 1980's. And the rotting remains of two wooden Landing Craft Infantry (Small), LCI(S), that had been converted into houseboats, are still to be seen on the mud beside the road at Bembridge creek on the Isle of Wight.

On 7th January 1946 Exbury House was recommissioned as HMS King Alfred. Throughout the war, King Alfred, which occupied Lancing College at Shoreham and premises at Hove, had been the main training 'ship' for cadet ratings under training as RNVR officers. Thousands of young men had passed through its portals before they were commissioned and posted to every kind of vessel in the Navy. Latterly it had become the main souce of supply of officers for major landing craft. But the rapid run-down of the Navy greatly reduced the need for officer cadets, and the continuing use of the premises at Lancing and Hove could not be justified. Whereas at its peak, the old King Alfred had seen weekly intakes of over 100 cadets, there were only 50 cadets altogether after the move to Exbury.

On 10th August 1946, King Alfred was paid off and was immediately recommissioned as HMS Hawke, a training school for ratings seeking commissions in the regular Navy. They were called Upper Yardsmen, and Exbury remained a training ship for them until 1st May 1955. On that day Hawke was paid off and Exbury House was returned to the Rothschild family.

The Beaulieu river had been de-requisitioned and returned to Lord Montagu on 28th February 1946, but

58. An LCI (L)

up to 1951 Buckler's Hard contained a maintenance yard for Motor Torpedo Boats and Harbour Defence Motor Launches. Latterly the yard was operated privately by James Wrann of Hythe during the period when the HDMLs were being used for ship-handling and navigation training by the cadet ratings of HMS Hawke.

Little visible evidence remains of the part the Beaulieu river played in the invasion of Europe, largely because in the intervening decades considerable efforts have been made to remove the traces of wartime disruption and restore the river to a peacetime state.

But somewhere near the mouth of the river, below Gins Farm, a pile of 7 cwt concrete blocks may still be lying on the river bed, a mute and unseen testimony to Nevil Shute's experiments with the launching trolley of the Swallow pilotless rocket aircraft. Upriver, off Clobb Copse, you can still see where Wates cut away a large slice of the river bank to float out the huge concrete floating dock. On each side of the opening the concrete face of the basin entrance is topped by a large concrete bollard, mute sentinels guarding the inlet, but the basin itself is silting up and is overhung by trees and saplings that have encroached to its very edges.

A mile further upstream, at Buckler's Hard, there

59. Former members of HMS Mastodon, HMS King Alfred and HMS Hawke dispersing after a service of commemoration at Exbury House, May 1992

remains a slipway where the naval artificers used to haul the American-built, British-manned LCVP assault boats out of the water to change their Chrysler engines and attend to damage to their hulls and propellers.

On the opposite side of the river, near the start of Gilbury pier, hidden by a tangle of bushes, is a small brick building once used by Mastodon as a cordage store, where the Wren trot boat crews used to huddle round a brazier between their journeys down-river to the major landing craft moorings. Apart from this, not a whisper remains of all those gallant young women, nor of the gallant young men who went to war from the Beaulieu river.

ABOUT THE AUTHOR

Cyril Cunningham is an experienced researcher. At the height of the Cold War he spent a decade working for various Defence Intelligence departments and for the Foreign Office Information Research Department. In 1954 he produced a detailed history for the War Office and the Air Ministry of the Communists' treatment of British prisoners of war in Korea.

In 1961 he left the Civil Service to practice as a psychologist in industry and later as a Senior Lecturer in the Portsmouth Management Centre.

He has contributed several feature articles to the Royal United Services Institute for Defence Studies and to the Times newspaper, and has also written a long list of papers and articles for learned professional journals and books, and for commercial journals and magazines. He has also spoken several times on Radio Solent and has appeared on television.

During the second world war, he joined the Navy in 1943 via the Cambridge University Naval Division and was commissioned as a Midshipman in the Royal Naval Volunteer Reserve shortly after his nineteenth birthday, in March 1944. On D-Day he was still undergoing gunnery training at Bognor Regis but soon afterwards saw active service in Normandy and later in North West Europe as the First Lieutenant of various tank landing craft. During the winter of 1944 he was attached to HMS Mastodon when his craft, LCT 2041, moored in the Beaulieu river.

In the autumn of 1945, at the end of the war with Japan, he made an epic voyage from Oban in Scotland to

60. The Author

Hong Kong in a 300 ton Infantry Landing Craft, surviving a typhoon in the South China Sea on the last leg of the voyage. He celebrated his survival and his twenty first birthday on arrival, in March 1946. He was demobilised six months later and returned to university to complete his studies.

He retired in 1988 after a long career as a Chartered Occupational Psychologist. He is married and has lived in Dibden Purlieu since 1961.

BIBLIOGRAPHY

Official Papers:
The Navy List
The Green List: Disposition of Landing Ships and Landing Craft
Public Records Office ADM. 210

Operations Orders:
Operation Neptune. Admiral Sir Betram Ramsey
J Force Orders Commodore G.N.Oliver,RN
G Force Orders Commodore C.E.Douglas-Pennant,RN.

British Vessels Lost at Sea 1939 - 45 H.M.S.O. Reprinted 1976 by Patrick Stephens.

Combined Operations:
The Watery Maze. Bernard Ferguson. 1966, Collins.
Assault from the Sea. Rear Admiral L.E.Maund. 1949 Metheun.
Destroyer Man. Rear Admiral A.F.Pugsley. 1957,Weidenfeld & Nicholson.

Landing Craft:
Quarterly Transactions of the Institution of Naval Architects 1947, Volume 89 No.3.
Warships of W.W.II: Part 8: Landing Craft. Lenton & College. 1964, Ian Allen.
Assault from the Sea. J.D.Ladd. 1976, David & Charles
The War of the Landing Craft. P.Lund & H.Ludman. 1976, New English Library
To Sea in a Seive. P.Bull. 1956, Corgi.

Commando:
The Beachhead Commandos. A.Cecil Hampshire. 1983, Wm. Kimber.

The Royal Marines. J.D.Ladd. 1982, Janes.
The Frogmen.Waldron & Gleeson. 1950, Evans.
The Commandos.Charles Messenger. 1985, Wm. Kimber.

History of World War II:
The Second World War.Winston.S.Churchill. 1952, Cassel & Co.
The Struggle for Europe.Chester Wilmot. 1953, Collins Son & Co.

Department of Miscellaneous Weapons Development:
The Secret War. Gerald Pawle. 1956, Harrup & Co. see also The Watery Maze

Mulberry Harbour:
Code Name Mulberry. Guy Hartcup. 1977, David & Charles.
Journal of the Civil Engineering Society, 1947

Nevil Shute:
Slide Rule. Nevil Shute. 1953, Wm. Heinemann.
Nevil Shute. Julian Smith. 1976, Twayne Publishers.
Requiem for a Wren. Nevil Shute. 1955, Wm. Heinemann Ltd.

Miscellaneous Works:
Battle of the Narrow Seas. Peter Scott. 1945, Country Life.
Operation Quicksilver. Peter Tooley. 1988, Ian Henry.
Springboard for Overlord. Anthony Kemp. 1984, Milestone Press.
Beaulieu in World War II. Walter Elsworth. 1982, Philpott Publications.
D-Day and the Beaulieu River. A.J.Holland. 1984.

APPENDIX

List of major landing craft using the Beaulieu River moorings during the Second World War:

AUGUST 1942

"A" SQUADRON
(Lieut-Commander Lord Beatty, R.N.)

2nd TLC(2) Flotilla
Craft Nos.
121, 124, 125,126, 127,
128,145, 163, 166, & 169

1st LCF Flotilla
Craft Nos.
2, 4, & 6

"B" SQUADRON
(Lieut-Commander H.Mulleneux, R.N.)

4th TLC(3)Flotilla
Craft Nos.
302, 303, 304,305,
306, 307, 308, 309, 310,
318, 325, 360, 361 & 376.

1st LCF Flotilla
Craft Nos.
1, 3, & 5

(All the above craft except TLC 128 took part in the Dieppe raid)

SEPTEMBER 1942

5th LCT(4) Flotilla
Craft Nos.
313, 314, 316, 317, 318,
321,322, 323, 324, 325,
342, & 354.

1st LCF Flotilla
Craft Nos. 1, 3, 4, 5, & 6

21st LCT(4) Flotilla
Craft Nos. not known

1943

3rd LCT Flotilla
Craft Nos. not known

5th LCT Flotilla
Craft Nos. not known

28th LCT(4) Flotilla
Craft Nos.
647, 749, 805,
808, 809,810
and others

33rd LCT(4) Flotilla
Craft Nos.
718, 719, 858, 878, 879,
897, and others.

37th LCT(4) Flotilla
Craft Nos.
567, 634, 639,700, 729, 938,
940, 941, 1006, & 1008.

JANUARY - D-DAY 1944

33rd LCT(4) Flotilla
Craft Nos. as above.

35th LCT(4) Flotilla
Craft Nos.
671, 721, 760, & 761.

36th LCT(4) Flotilla
Craft Nos.
672, 673, 770,932, 934,
935, & 936.

37th LCT(4) Flotilla
Craft Nos. as above.
plus LCF 4.

28th LCT(4) Flotilla
Craft Nos. as above.

332nd SUPPORT SQUADRON (G) FORCE

LCF(Mark 4)
Craft Nos.
19, 20, 25 26, 35, 36,
and 38.

LCG(L) (Mark 3)
Craft Nos.
1, 2, 3, 13, 17, & 18.

ROCKET CRAFT - LCT(R)
Craft Nos.
362, 434, 435, 436,438, 440, 459 & 460.

Mk 5 LCT ASSAULT FLOTILLAS

108th Flotilla
Craft Nos.
2005, 2226, 2233, 2238,
2262, 2266,
2442 & 2499.

109th Flotilla
Craft Nos.
2039, 2048, 2121, 2225,
2236, 2291,
2345 & 2453.

AFTER D-DAY.

LCF
Craft Nos.
19, 20, 26, 32, 36 and 38.

LCG(L)
Craft Nos.
2, 3, 11, 13, 17, 18.764
and 680.

ROCKET CRAFT LCT(R)
Craft Nos.
405, 428 and 460

Mk. 5 LCTs (Various Flotillas)
Craft Nos.
2005, 2011, 2041, 2044, 2047,
2079, 2121, 2192, 2226, 2232,
2270, 2292, 2313, 2427, 2453,
2477 and 2479.

Abbreviations:
TLC ......Tank Landing Craft (early version of LCT)
LCT ......Landing Craft Tank: figures in brackets are the Mark
   numbers e.g. (3) = Mark 3
LCF ......Landing Craft Flak
LCG(L) .Landing Craft Gun (Large)
LCT(R) ..Landing Craft Tank (Rocket) also known as Rocket Craft.

INDEX

Aircraft:
Doodlebugs 64
JU 188 40,44
Swallow pilotless
aircraft 4,42,43,45,46,72

HM Ships and Shore Establishments:
H.M.S. Bee 31
Bulolo 51
Calpe 14
Chinkara 63
Dinosaur 11
Erebus 59,60
Grey Goose 31
Invicta 65
Hawke 71,72
Jervis 27
Jamaica 70
King Alfred 41,71
Kingsmill 60
Lawford 35,51,53,54
Mastodon 1-4,11, 15-17,28-39, 40-46,49-57, 60-63,68,70-72
Medina 9,18
Northney 8
Roberts 59,60
Squid 17,32,56,62
Tormentor 8,56,64
Vectis 17,27
Warspite 32,59,60
X 20 & X23,
(midget submarines) 35

Landing Craft Flotillas and Units:
"A" Squadron TLC 11,13,16
Ancillary Flotilla 476,39,50
"B" Squadron TLC 11,13
"B" Squadron LCVP 39,50-52
Calshot Naval Unit 30
Ferry Units 9,30,48
Flotilla 813 LCVP 57
G Force Support
Squadron 37-39,50,51
J Force Support Squadron 32
LCF No.1 Flotilla 18
Support Flotilla 332,50

Support Squadron Eastern Flank
(SSEF) 55,59,62,70

LCT Flotilla Nos:
2nd 11,15,16
4th 11,15,18
5th 15,16,18
21st 16,18
28th see appendix
33rd 32
35th 32
36th see appendix
37th 34
102nd 57,63
103rd see appendix
106th 57
107th 57
108th 38,50,57,63
109th 38,50

LCT Nos:
121 15
124 15
126 15,56
128 15,16
145 15
159 15
161 23,24
789 61
868 2
2041 58
3626 57

LC Flak Nos:
1 3,12-14,16,55
2 12,13,15
3 13,16
4 13,16,18,32
5 13,16,18
6 13,16
18 56
19 37,56
20 37,56
25 37
26 37,56
32 56,61
35 37
36 37,56,60
38 37,56,60

LC Gun (Large) Nos:
1 37
2 37,56,60,61
3 37,56
11 56,61
13 37,56
15 65
16 65
17 37,56,61
18 37,56
680 56
764 56

LC Gun (Medium) Nos:
101 61
102 61

LCT (Rocket) Nos:
161 23,24
362 37,50
405 53
428 see appendix
434 37
436 37
438 37,56
440 37,50
459 37,50
460 37,50,56

LCH No:
98 60

Minor Landing Craft:
Landing Barge Kitchen
(LBK) 9,30,47
Landing Barge Vehicle
(LBV) 9,16,18,29,48
Minca Barges 9
Landing Craft Assault
(LCA) 7,8,63
Landing Craft Assault
(Hedgerow) 41,52
Landing Craft Mechanised
(LCM) 7,8,30,48
Landing Craft Vehicle/
Personnel (LCVP) 2,26,30,31, 39,48,50,52, 56,57,72
Landing Craft Personnel
Ramped (LCPR) 39,50

Motor Gun Boats/Torpedo Boats:
MGB 312 36
316 36
317 36
324 36
326 36
330 36

MTB 55th Flotilla 37

J Class Minesweepers: 8

Mulberry Harbour Units:
Beetles 21,22
Bombardons 20
Intermediate Pontoons 22
Mulberry Harbour 15,19,20,22, 24,26,30,55, 65,67
Phoenix's 20,53

Other Naval & Military Units:
Beach Signals No.3. 11,35
Bombardment Units 34,35,51
Bureau Central de
Renseignements (BCRA -
Free French SOE) 23
Canadian
Commando 14,39,50,59
Combat Parachute
Company (Free French) 23
Combined Operations
Pilotage Parties (COPPs) 35-37
Dept of Miscellaneous
Weapons Development
(DMWD) 24,34,41-43
G Force 27,34,37,38,47-49,56
J Force (Dieppe Raid) 14,17
J Force 27,32,34,36-38,47.63
Landing CraftObstacle
Clearance Units
(LCOCU) 35,36,49
Landing Craft Repair
and Recovery Units
(LCRRU) 36
"L" RN Commando 35
Naval Party 1734 63
Naval Party 1740 63

78

"P" RN Commando	35,39,44	
Pioneer Corps	25,26	
Royal Army Service Corps	30	
Royal Canadian Navy	34	
Royal Corps of Naval Constructors	10,24	
Royal Engineers	35	
Royal Marines	13,26,30,34, 35,39,49-51, 59.61,65,68	
Small Scale Raiding Force (SSRF)	4,23	
Special Operations Executive (SOE)	4,22,23,67	
Womens Royal Army Corps (WRAC)- formerly the ATS	64	
Womens Royal Naval Service (WRNS)	1,2,26-29,32, 39,40,49,50-53, 63,68-70	

Personnel:

Aisher, Sir Owen	18,22
Beatty, Earl, Lt. Cdr. RN	11,12,16
Bull Peter Lt. RNVR	11
Cavendish Susan, Petty Officer WRNS	69,70
Cheney Arthur Lt. RNVR	3,15,56,60,61
Churchill Winston	6,8,9
Clarke C.R. Lt. Cdr. RN	31,68
Dalton Alan (later Sir Alan) Sub/Lt. RNVR	35
Dodd D.H. Flt Sgt. RAF	44
Dolphin G.V.M. Capt RN	34,49
Douglas-Pennant C.E. Cdre. RN	33,49
Downer Frank	19
Dreyer C. Cdr. RN	36
Dudley N.M. 2nd Officer WRNS	70
Fanshaw A.B. Capt. RN	32,33
Firth Joan, WRNS	68
Forster, Lady	6,28
Green Allan SBA	11
Hassan V.C. Surg. Lt. RNVR	11
Henbury A. Surg. Lt. RNVR	11
Hughes-Hallett J. Cdre. RN	3,14,15,17,19,23,70
Irvine P.M. 3rd Officer WRNS	68
Keyes Sir Roger, Admiral of the Fleet	8,9
King George VIth	39
Langley F.H.G. Colonel	23
Macglashen Lt. Cdr. RCNVR	11
Maud C. Capt. RN	35
McLaughlin P.V. Capt. RN	36
Miller Vera Regulating P.O. WRNS	70
Montagu Lord	6,8,42,71
Montgomery Sir Bernard, General	37
Moore A.D. Vice Admiral	27
Mountbatten Earl	4,9,14,17,19
Mulleneux H. Lt. Cdr. RN	11
Norway Nevil Shute Lt. Cdr. RNVR	1,24,40-46, 53,65,72
Oliver G.N. Cdre. RN	27,49
Otway-Ruthven R.J. Capt. RN	32,34
Paule G.	41
Pleydell-Bouverie, Capt. the Hon.	8
Pope R.K.C. Cdr. RN	28,31
Price G.D. Lt. RNVR	36
Prior R.M. Cdr. RN	3,28,60
Pugsley A.F. Capt. RN	3,27,28, 33,49,53,54, 59,60,62,65, 66,70
Ramsey Sir Bertram, Admiral	7,27,49,59,70
Robinson H.S. Lt. Cdr. RNVR	17,18,28
Rothschild Edmund de.	3
Rothschild Lionel de	3,10
Ryder R.E.D., VC, Cdr. RN	3,32,65,70
Saunders A.V. Fl. Lt. RAF	44
Scott P (later Sir Peter) Lt. Cdr. RNVR	31
Sellar K.A. Cdr. RN	3,55,60,62,70
Shute Nevil	see Norway
Smith Ena WRNS	18
Smith Julian	41
Spreadbury B. WRNS	18
Stirling W. Colonel	23
Swinley R. Capt. RN	31, 39,41,51,54, 59,65,66,68,70
Thompson Betty, Regulating P.O. WRNS	70
Vian, Sir Phillip, Rear Admiral	54
Wates Ltd. Civil Engineers	18,21,72
Watson Jean, WRNS	3,51

Places:

All Saints Church, Fawley	44
Antwerp	57,59,62
Bailey's Hard	4,6,8,9,18,25, 28,29
Beaulieu Spit	7
Boulogne	57,58
Bucklers Hard	4,6-9,18,25,26, 28,29,36,39,57,72
Calshot Spit	30,49
Clobb Copse	7,9,18,20,21, 22,26,72
Clob Gorse	22
Dibden Bay	4,22
Dieppe	3,4,11,12,14,15,17, 19,23,28,31,32,34, 42,55-57,65
Dolphin Hotel, Southampton	66
Domus, Beaulieu	67
Dunkirk	7,8,27,57
Exbury House	1,4,6,10,11, 13,18,28,29,34, 35,43,44,49,51, 68,70,71
Exbury Church	35
Gilbury Hard	6,10,13,39
Gilbury House	4,6,28
Gilbury Pier	6,36,39,49-51,72
Gins Quay	10
House by the Shore	22
Husbands Shipyard	8,22
Hythe Marina	22
Inchmery House	6,10,22
Lepe	20,25,28,38
Lepe House	4,6,25,28-29, 32,35,37,49,70
Marchwood	19,20
Master Builder's House Hotel	4,25,28,39,57
Montagu Arms Hotel	4,29,50,63,67,68,70
Needs Oar Point	7,22,36,42,43
Northam, Southampton	65
Ostend	58,59
Oyster Beds, Beaulieu River	18-20
Palace House	6,22
Park Farm	22
Q Hard, Lepe	29,38,50
Star Hotel, Southampton	66
Southampton	29,32,34,38, 45,50,51
The Drokes	22
The Rings	22
Walcheren Island	28,56,58, 59-62
Warren Flat	7
Warren House	22
Westkapelle	59,60
Weston Super Mare	43
West Scheldt	59,62,63
White Horse Hotel, Romsey	70
Worthy Down	43

79